The travels of a Usher

© 2020, Dangleterre, Sandrine
Edition : Books on Demand,
12/14 rond-Point des Champs-Elysées, 75008 Paris
Impression : BoD - Books on Demand, Norderstedt, Allemagne
ISBN : 9782322139255
Dépôt légal : novembre 2020

Sandrine Dangleterre

The travels of a Usher

Prologue

I grew up unknowingly with a progressive disease; I had Usher Syndrome, but I didn't know it. I have therefore lived from birth with total deafness, then with a progressive loss of the visual field.

A few years ago, many did not believe me capable of traveling alone or in a group, or of playing sports, studying ... But they were very wrong for lack of information, because I was able to do all this despite the disease.

Finally I take the pen to prove to you that it is possible to live like everyone else and to tell my story, my experiences, through different trips that I have made in the world, presenting of course anecdotes, but also obstacles to which I have always found solutions.

I have traveled a lot, I have fond memories, I have had beautiful and very enriching experiences. I chose a few countries because I couldn't tell you all about them.

The most important thing that you are going to discover is how I gradually came to realize my disease, what the evolution of this disease has been, and especially this ability to live like everyone else and to discover each country. I was so marked by all these experiences, all these strong emotions felt during these trips, that I remember everything perfectly.

I only discovered the name of my disease when I was 30; it was very late, especially since I had realized for a long time that I did not see like the others. Before I turned 30, people always laughed at me, blaming me for being "in the moon".

From the moment I found out about my illness, people adapted to me and respected me more.

Currently, information is gradually circulating about this rare disease, but it is still unknown.

Chapter 1

Greece - 1986

My sister and brother's college organized a trip to Greece and my parents fought for me to attend; it was during the Easter holidays, two weeks outside of school time.

In addition, I was still attending the Education Center for Deaf Youth (CEJS) in Arras. Finally, college accepted me. It was my first time on a trip with my brother's and sister's school, especially being integrated with hearing college students. I'll tell you about this trip, but I only have vague memories of it because it was a long time ago.

In Athens, the capital of Greece, we visited the "Parthenon" a building located on the Acropolis of Athens and made of marble. I can't tell you more because the guide spoke and no one translated me into sign language or spoken. The view from the "Parthenon" impressed me.
We went to admire the capital from the top of a hill; in fact, we saw a big black cloud, it was pollution; it's a shame because we weren't able to admire the city well; I still tried to take a picture,

even though it was not pretty to see, I had no choice.

Located 169 km from Athens, Delphi is one of the most important archaeological sites in Greece. Sanctuary common to all the cities of ancient Greece, Delphi had considerable religious influence.

Nestled on one of the sides of Mount Parnassus, this sanctuary dedicated to Apollo and which is characterized by the presence of an oracle where a pythia officiated, enjoys a splendid panorama over the valley with, on the horizon, the gulf. of Corinth. The temple of Apollo and the theater, which date from the 4th century BC. AD, are remarkable beauty.

The site of Olympia, in a valley of the Peloponnese, was inhabited since prehistoric times, and the cult of Zeus was established there from the tenth century BC. In addition to the temples, there are remains of all the sports facilities for the celebration of the Olympic Games which were held there every four years from 776 BC. J.-C.

At the end of the fortnight, I felt excluded from this group due to my deafness: I had difficulty reading the lips of college students and teachers because the conversations were moving too quickly.

Like tennis, and also I couldn't know who was speaking; It made me so tired to run over their lips to follow the communication, luckily I enjoyed the visits, but without being able to access the information or the explanations, too bad.

I discovered the different cultures between hearing and deaf, especially the hearing school, the deaf school and also sports clubs.
This trip to Greece introduced me to a different culture, beautiful landscapes and made me want to know other countries; afterwards, my dream was to go as far as possible, that is to say to Australia.

Chapter 2

China - 1991

It was my first distant trip, fifteen hours of non-stop flight with seven hours of jet lag and above all with a group of thirty-six French and Swiss oral deaf people aged twenty to eighty-four.

At Roissy Charles de Gaulle, I arrived by the shuttle coming from the metro, I looked for the number where the manager of Fugues et Loisirs named Huguette had given me an appointment. I was very shy, I didn't dare ask if this was the right group; luckily I spotted a cover, the same one I had been given in advance; So it was the right group, I was relieved but I had to wait a bit because I had arrived too early. Suddenly someone from the group questioned me orally :
- Are you a participant in the trip to China ?
- Yes ! I replied briefly, seeing my shyness.
- Ok come on! I introduce you to the manager.
- Ok, I follow you !
- This is Huguette, responsible for the trip.
- Hello Huguette.
- Hello what is your name ?
- Sandrine Dangleterre.

Huguette found my name in the list of participants.
- It is good and welcome among us, come and stay with the others; OK ?
- OK and thank you.

In front of the group, I said hello to them quickly without introducing myself due to a mixture of anxiety, shyness and unease, but happy to fly to China. It was my grandparents who gave me this beautiful gift.

During the flight, I was well installed near the corridor, but I found it embarrassing to be in this place because a lot of people or hostesses passed by and it prevented me from sleeping or focus to look at the screen at the bottom. For a while when it was time to sleep, the lights went out; I was then a little panicked because I wanted to go to the toilet and I couldn't see anything at all; I moved my head to try to find a solution, and spotted little lights on the floor only in the hallway. After a few minutes I still didn't dare go to the bathroom, unfortunately my bladder was completely full, so I had to take my courage in both hands to go. I had an idea: I was going to feel the seats and count them to the toilet; so I went for it. I calculated the number of seats, one, two, three, four, five, six, seven, phew! I didn't bump into it. Hop! In the bathroom I emptied my bladder, it relieved me then, on my return, I did the same, I counted one, two, three, four, five, six, seven. And I said to myself: " Shit ! What seat exactly? In front of ? Or behind? "; I stood for a few minutes to find my exact seat. I pretended to loosen my legs, like a little gymnastics, while taking my time to find my real seat. I still had an idea, I felt with my foot to see if the seat was empty or not; alas! I felt there was a foot, the front seat was taken, so my seat was behind; I settled in with relief but it annoyed me.

On arrival in Beijing, the capital of China, the weather was very muggy, very humid, over thirty-five degrees and his watch added seven hours.

In the restaurant, we sat around a round table, with a small trolley in the middle where various dishes were without drinks; it was convenient to rotate the small table to help yourself freely while still seated. I was so thirsty for the heat! The waiter came to our table and asked us in English:
- What would you like to drink ?
- Still water ! I replied in English.
- Unfortunately there is only sparkling water.
- Is that so ! So nothing for me and thank you.

One of the deaf saw that I was speaking English, but not fluent, only words; so he begged me to translate for their drink orders; I helped them out, then another deaf one asked me:

- Please ask the waiter what are the dishes on the small rolling table.
- OK ! I told them.
- Sir, what are these dishes? I translated to the server.
- Beef, noodles, soup etc....
- Thank you !
- Enjoy your meal !
- Why do you want to know what these dishes are ? I dared to ask one of the deaf.
- I heard that in Asia, we eat cats, dogs, rats etc. ...
- You're kidding ?
- No, it's true and we'll go and ask the guide to find out if it's true or not.
- OK !
- Sir, do the Chinese or Asians eat dogs, cats, rats etc. ? one of us asked the guide accompanied by Huguette.
- Yes it is, but not everywhere; here we are in restaurants adapted to foreigners so everything is fine.
- Ah damn ! Beurkkk !! we said.

It's misery !!

We took the road to the hotel to drop off our suitcases at reception; Huguette asked us to listen to her carefully :

- Okay, I'll explain the program for today: meet here in half an hour to go on a visit; OK ?
- Yes !
- Here is a flag that will help us follow each other without getting lost and please stay in a group.
- Yes !
- Well, I call you by your first names to give you the keys two by two; We're hurrying, so listen to me carefully.
- Yes.
- Sandrine.
- Present.
- With Catherine.
- Uh ! Who is Catherine ? I said.
- The ! Hop ! The elevator is on the right.

    The call continued, I dropped my suitcase in the bedroom. Chic ! Half an hour had passed, everyone had introduced themselves, and, with the Chinese guide, we left to visit the « Temple of Heaven »; this temple was a monument of Beijing, located in the historic district of Xuanwu in the south of the city. It was considered the pinnacle of traditional Chinese architecture. Its layout symbolizes the Chinese belief that the earth is square and the sky round.
    The guide asked us :
- How many nails are in this temple of heaven
- Two million ?
- A thousand ?

- No.
- More ? Or less ?
- Less.
- Huh ! Uh two hundred ?
- No.
- No ? I replied.
- There, good answer.
- Not possible ! For the frame, we need nails to hang the tiles…
- It is true ! But here no need, look closely. It was a little dark for me to see well; too bad, I did my best to see everything and also I traded with a few deaf; it was like I saw almost everything.
- Ah darn ! It's true, to hang frames and candles we used threads! I sighed.
- Yes ! Fair ! And the frame ?
- Timber that fits together.
- Yes ! Well.

Then we visited « Tian An Men » Square; the guide explained to us :
- The "Tian An Men" square is full of strong emotions due to the death of Hu Yaobang who was run over by a tank. The Tian An Men protests took place between April 15 and June 4, 1989, in this very square. They ended with a wave of repression, sometimes included under the expression "massacre of" Tian An Men square. They took the form of a movement of Chinese students, intellectuals and workers, denouncing cor-

ruption and calling for political and democratic reforms.

I heard this story from the news with subtitles on TV, it was a big shock to the world. China is a communist country.

In this square, a group of schoolgirls all dressed in the same tracksuits sang the Chinese hymn as they walked in pairs like the military. Many groups of tourists of different nationalities were walking around and photographing without straying from their groups because the rules are strict. For example, it was forbidden to go outside this place to visit the slums or elsewhere, we had to respect the visit routes, and the Chinese military kept watch. Around this place, on the road, cyclists circulated and there were few cars; pedestrians had difficulty crossing, we had to cross quickly and zigzagging between bikes which did not give priority to pedestrians.

One of us asked the guide :
- It's amazing how many cyclists there are !
- Yes, a car is expensive here, and even a bicycle! said the guide.
- A bicycle is not expensive ?
- No, but for them it is expensive: a bicycle costs 200 yuan and a monthly salary is about 20 yuan.

- Ah ! To have a bike, you have to work for 10 months !
- Yes.

On the way to the "Great Wall", it was market day: all the buses were going slowly, including ours; those who were sitting by the bus window saw everything that happened. A poor Chinese man stole a vegetable, two soldiers grabbed him, put their hands behind his back and beat him in front of everyone; it was a shock for tourists !

One of us asked for water; so we went down to buy bottles of water; the guide warned us :
- Pay attention ! And make sure the bottles haven't been opened. Its good ?
- Why ? one of us said.
- Because in China, water is not drinkable; if the bottles have already been opened, then they may have filled them with non-potable water, which they sell to us, and we may get sick.
- How to check ?
- You take a bottle, you try to unscrew the cap; if it's hard, it's good; and if it spins easily, it has already been opened; so you give it back by refusing it and you take another bottle. OK ?
- Oh ok !
- It's the same, at the hotel, avoid using tap water to brush your teeth.
- Oh ok !
  - Follow me ! said the guide.

At the market, I bought two one-and-a-half-liter water bottles, checking that the bottles were new, then I drank a bottle completely, slowly, I was so thirsty and also because I had no nothing drunk for a day and a half; It did me good. I put a cold bottle in my backpack, knowing that the water would be hot quickly from the heat; but that was okay: at the hotel there was a small fridge with a small freezer, so in the evening I put it in the freezer, it would stay fresh all day.

We then went to visit "The Great Wall", one of the greatest wonders in the world. The Chinese guide told us the story of The Great Wall :
- Literally "the long wall" is a set of Chinese military fortifications built, destroyed and rebuilt in several times and in several places between the 3rd century BC and the 17th century to mark and defend the northern border of China. It is the most important architectural structure ever built by man both in length, area and mass.
- How many kilometers is this wall? asked a deaf one.
- Its length is approximately 6500 km.
- Height and width ?
- 6 to 7 m high, and 4 to 5 m wide.
- It's huge to have been doing this for 15 centuries! I exclaimed.

It's amazing and unimaginable to have built this great wall by hand, without cranes, concrete mixers etc. We walk in and I say to myself: wow! The path is straight, without a switchback, although there are hills, mountains or rice fields; so the slope is steep and the view is magnificent.

The guide told us about a nice surprise that was not written in the program :
- Tonight, meet at the hotel reception at 7:00 p.m. to go to the circus show.
- Oh nice ! we exclaimed.

Deep inside, I felt stuck because walking around in the dark made me nervous.

Luckily, two elderly ladies, M and T, asked me to go with them because they were scared, and I accepted right away, I was saved.

Afterwards, at the show, it was impressive! Flexibility, balancing act, acrobats, aerobatics, hands to hands, Kung Fu: very young artists who were of very high level, with physical and mental qualities and above all, the most extraordinary, the spectacle of the dragon who I liked.

While visiting the "Tombs of the Mings", I saw tombs which are on either side of a sacred path,

an avenue in the middle of the tomb area; on either side of this avenue we discovered statues of stone animals: camels, lions, dragons, turtles etc. The Chinese guide told us :
- The Imperial Cemetery covers an area of 120 square kilometers and thirteen of the sixteen emperors of the Ming Dynasty are buried there in a necropolis. The Mings Dynasty ruled China from 1368 to 1644. This represents the largest number of emperors in a Chinese imperial necropolis.

During the ride, I noticed that a woman in her thirties, the tallest in our group, was still hanging on a person's arm due to a balance problem and I wondered what she had. I didn't dare ask him, but maybe someday.

I spoke with a few people a bit because I was reserved and shy, but it was going well for me, slowly, to get to know our group better; besides, I was the youngest; Also, it had been a long time since I had seen deaf people since I had studied (high school and university) with hearing people, without a sign language interpreter.

I laughed because a few people told me :
- We learned that your first name was Sandrine and we thought you were a young man because of your outfits and your somewhat mas-

culine behavior; and also we were surprised that you share your room with Catherine: indeed we thought you were engaged.
- Ah! Hee hee! No, I didn't know Catherine!
- Now we know that you are indeed a woman and uh! Are you athletic considering your broad shoulders? Which sports do you practice?
- Judo, I am a first Dan black belt, tennis and swimming.
- Are you studying?
- Yes, I am a first year DEUG student in STAPS in Lille.
- STAPS? What's this?
- Technical Sciences of Sports Physical Activities.
- Ah! What will you do after your studies
- Sports teacher.
- Wow! Well done and good luck!
- Thank you.

Sometimes a few deaf people got angry with me because when they called me with signs in the air, I did not see them and they said to me :
- Why are you running away? Or are you ignoring us?
- No, I'm not running away, I focus on the visits, that fascinates me, that's all.
- Weird, it looks like you are head in the air.
- Ah! Possible, I am often in the moonlight and it is better to pat myself on the shoulder.

- Oh ok !

I thought: Phew! No conflicts. I don't understand why I am often in the moon, yet I am careful; It annoys me and I always have to find good excuses to avoid anger or controversy. But the others see well when they are called and waved in the air; not me, pff! Does that mean I'm not like the others ?

We visited the "Summer Palace", rich in one of the most beautiful imperial parks with its pavilions. On this site was Longevity Hill and Kunming Lake. The whole covers an area of 2.9 km2, three-quarters of which is occupied by a body of water. On the 70,000 m2 of built area, there is a great diversity of gardens, palaces and other buildings of classical Chinese style. We strolled admiring the park, very calm, like zen; I spotted Chinese people playing Chinese checkers and Chinese goose, it was complicated; I tried to guess the rules, without success; I couldn't ask them because they didn't speak French or English and didn't understand mimes; It's a shame because I love board games.

Kunming Lake is crossed by the Seventeen Arch Bridge; built in masonry between 1751 and 1764, it has a pedestrian bridge.

At the restaurant, I always sat down at the round table in the middle of which was a small revolving table, it often happened to me that people accuse me of behaving like a savage unable to control his gluttony because I was shooting the small table without paying attention to the others who had not finished serving themselves; yet I was trying very hard to avoid this; but it wasn't easy for me. All this criticism annoyed me more and more in secret.

Here I am at the "Forbidden City" which is the imperial palace within the Imperial City of Beijing, made very famous by the film « The Last Emperor » made in 1987. This Forbidden City, also called the Palace Museum, extends over an area of 72 ha including 50 ha of gardens; it is one of the oldest and best preserved palaces in China and, according to legend, has 9,999 rooms.

The construction of the Forbidden City took 14 years and more than a million enslaved workers are said to have worked there. A first palace was completed in 1420 but burned down in 1424. Between 1420 and 1911, a total of 24 emperors resided there. Before 1924, when it was opened to the public, no one other than the Emperor and his court was allowed to approach or even look at it. Private pavilions belonged to the imperial family and the concubines.

One morning, one of us asked Huguette orally and in sign language to ask the guide a question, then Huguette translated to the guide :
- Are there associations of the deaf ?
- Uh ! Yes.
- Can we see them ?
- I will try to contact some so that we can visit the deaf but I can not guarantee you anything.
- Great thanks and do your best.

I did not see these conversations, and only learned about them when I visited the facility for the deaf.

In front of the huge armored doors like a safe, I was shocked and speechless; at the reception, the carpet was all red, two soldiers gave us orders and then Huguette translated :
- Do not move away, stay in a group and do not make noise so as not to disturb those who work; it's clear ?
- Yes !
- The rules are very strict here !
- Pay attention please! whispered Huguette to us.
- If we don't play by the rules, what will happen ?
- They'll kick us out immediately.
- Oh okay, oh that's really very strict! I said to myself.

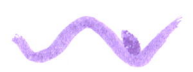

The first large room, all red, still with red carpets and red curtains, was the meeting room; it was quite cold with a long, simple rectangular table and simple wooden chairs with a portrait of the dictator on the wall; the second room was still red, all red because it is a communist country, workers without legs were seated on the ground or on wooden crutches for those who had one less leg; the third room was huge, with several rows of long tables. I guessed that people with various disabilities were working there in the assembly line doing packaging etc. It looked like a CAT in France. We then arrive in front of Chinese deaf people; One of them called me in secret and asked me in Chinese Sign Language some questions that I tried to understand with the help of a deaf Swiss :
- Are you deaf ?
- Yes.
- Where are you from ?
- France. (I mimed the rooster).
- Ah ! Okay and are you a boy?
- I don't, a woman.
- Ah! Okay, I thought you were a boy.

Some deaf French people laughed while keeping watch to protect us; my Chinese interlocutor was thirsty to communicate with me :
- Do you cycle in France ?

- Yes all deaf people have them, and you ?
- No, never, it is forbidden to leave the establishment, it is dangerous for us and you drive a car ?
- Yes we drive.

Suddenly, a deaf man, seeing a leader arriving, motioned for us to stop the conversation; we pretended to watch the workers, and the Chinese continued to work; phew! We were saved and my Chinese interlocutor thanked us. When we left the establishment, we spoke to each other a bit because we had some trouble.

I was lost in my thoughts, speechless, in shock like other deaf people: poor Chinese deaf; this establishment was like a prison for the handicapped, I did not accept that; fortunately, in France it was not like that. They were not enjoying their life, it must be hard for them, but they told us they were happy because they ate well and felt protected inside the facility.

The guide then told us :
- We go to the market, outside the city, stay in a group because it is easy to get lost.

At the market, the smell was unpleasant, I had trouble breathing, especially with the heat in addition, I saw lots of cages with cats, turtles, dogs inside... I said to myself "they will what? I was shocked to see a cat dealer take a live cat, knock it out, then put it in a pot full of boiling water for a few minutes; then he would take it out, cut it out to tear off the skin, and cut it up.

   A deaf man said to me :
- Here ! I told you from day one.
- Yes I see, the proof is there, it's horrible, poor cats and dogs. It was the same in France, formerly during the First World War, the French, very poor and hungry, hunted rats to survive.
- Exact ! Life is hard but hey ...

   Visit of a "lamas temple"; the guide summarized us :
- Literally, it is the « Palace of Peace and Harmony », a temple of Tibetan Buddhism in Beijing founded in 1694, under the Qing dynasty. One of the statues, which reaches a height of twelve meters, represents a Buddhist standing.

   We then flew 1074 kilometers from Beijing to Xian, the ancient capital of many dynasties, with more than thirty centuries of history; we visited the Great Wild Goose Pagoda which was built between 707 and 709 with the Drum Tower contrasting with the Bell Tower as the bell was once struck at dawn while the drum was being beaten at sunset, indicating the end of the day.

At lunchtime, at the restaurant table, I spoke to the waiter as usual :
- Hello.
- Hello in Chinese (I think)
- What are these dishes ?

The waiter smiled at me without understanding
- Do you speak English or French ?

The waiter smiled at me again without understanding. So I announced to the whole table:
- Unfortunately, this waiter cannot speak English or French.
- Ah darn !
- Stuck up.
- So we'll call the guide.
- OK Go ahead ! did I say.

A deaf man went to get the guide with Huguette to translate and came back to our table after asking them :
- These dishes?
- Ah! This is eel soup, this is beef etc. ...
- Thank you ! we exclaimed.

I have observed well; especially the eel soup which struck me as weird, and which I didn't want to taste, especially since I don't really like fish. Everyone had a great time, the dishes were almost all empty.

Huguette asked me for a favor :
- Please, can you go with Nicole ?
- Excuse me, who is Nicole? I don't know all the first names yet.
- This woman, come and let me introduce you.
- With pleasure !
- Here is Nicole and here is Sandrine! Huguette said, introducing us to each other.
- Hello Nicole ! I replied to Nicole.
- Hello Sandrine, I can't see very well and thank you for agreeing to come with me.
- You're welcome and with pleasure.
- And thank you also for speaking softly and well in front of me.
- Ok no problem, I can repeat it if you don't understand; OK ! I smile.

I wondered how I was going to accompany it: indeed, I had watched it work since the start of the trip; so I managed to be careful; it was the first time that I accompanied Nicole; she had her arm hooked to mine and I was walking slowly because I knew she had balance issues; it was not easy because I also have balance problems myself, but they are minor.

We visited the "Mausoleum of Emperor Qin Shi Huang Di" and "Lintong excavation sites" where there is buried a terracotta army, a clay army made up of more than six thousand statues of horsemen and infantry that the emperor had executed in life size; and the whole stretches for about 56.25 square kilometers, with many wooden or iron stairs and very narrow paths. I have gave Nicole in her hands all the information to let her know that there were steps to go down or up and also to get behind me; everything went well, I realized that it required a lot of attention and work from Nicole to avoid falling or hurting her ... And the fact that Huguette wanted to share the accompanying Nicole was a good idea: it was nice to share and help Nicole out of solidarity; I consider Nicole like everyone else, she just needs some guidance and I had no trouble communicating with her, I helped her wholeheartedly; for me it was quite normal.

At the "Hot Springs" of Huanqing which are located thirty kilometers east of Xian at the foot of Lishan Mountain, the paths were dirt, so not flat; it took a lot of work to guide Nicole, the worst part was the badly laid stone stairs: I almost lost my balance guiding her because she had big balance problems but I managed to hold on right and I was reassured that we did not fall; it was not obvious in this dense crowd, as I was guiding Nicole without losing sight of our group and while trying to enjoy the visit; it was not a good experience for me.

The guide gave us a summary :
- These sources were discovered 3,000 years ago. Most of the dynasties that took Xian as their capital established a pleasure park around the hot springs that spring up on the northern slope of Lishan Mountain. It has been a spa site for thousands of years; Today you can still go there to the thermal springs and bathe in the mineral and limpid waters which are at a temperature of 43 degrees.
- Wow ! Forty-three degrees! It makes me want to swim! I exclaimed.
- Hi! No time to swim, we continue the visit.
- Pity !

The "Forest of Steles" or the Beilin museum is a prestigious collection bringing together writings on stone by the greatest writers of China. The stelae bear the texts which formed the basis of teaching under the Han dynasty. It is possible to purchase hard copies of the stelae, made by ink transfer.

Departure for Luoyang by train, six hours of travel for a distance of three hundred and seventy-seven kilometers; the train was therefore traveling at a speed of 40 to 50 kilometers per hour.

In this wild site formed by a gorge of the Yi River, I admired one of the most beautiful jewels of Buddhist art in China. From the late 5th century until the 11th century, generations of stonemasons and sculptors dug caves and grottoes and excavated the stone to make nearly one hundred thousand statues of Buddha.

Departure for Sushou by train; more than sixteen hours of travel for a distance of nine hundred and forty kilometers: we were therefore going to have dinner and sleep in the sleeper train, six people per cabin; Huguette called us by our first names for each cabin: I found myself with five men; Oh my God ! I didn't accept and went to see Huguette to find out why ?
- Huguette, you know that I am a woman, not a man; so why am I sleeping with five men? You exaggerate.
- I understand your annoyance, but the problem is that there is one extra woman, so I chose you because you are very athletic.
- Yes, but still !
- I know but these five men are very nice; don't worry, and please, it's for one night only.
- Ok, I have no choice; that's it ?
- Yes, I'm so sorry.
- OK I understand.

When I got back to my cabin, I said to the five men :

- First, I choose my bed, so I take the highest.
- OK no problem !

With my bladder full, I looked for a bathroom. When I entered it, I did not find a basin; Ah darn ! I looked on the ground, ah! Here is a hole: we could see the wooden sleepers which were linked to the rails; my God ! I was digging around the hole to see if anyone was below. I was urinating quickly, because I was not comfortable, and at the same time I was careful not to drop things and also to aim well in the hole, not easy for women and also the train was moving too much.

The night train journey was painful because it went very slowly; there was no air conditioning, the heat weighed on us and exhausted us. When night fell, I had a hard time falling asleep because at each stop the train gave me funny vibrations and also because of the heat that was suffocating us.

The sun rose, the landscapes were flooded, covered with water; I went to see the guide with Huguette to ask them :
- What is happening ? It's flooded everywhere.
- Yes, we escaped a disaster because a typhoon passed the old woman.
- Ah ! Phew ! And here there are often typhoons ?

- Yes, during the monsoons, especially in August.
- Oh my God ! In Suzhou it's flooded ?
- No, it's next door.

Finally, we arrived in Suzhou, which was the city of water, golden mists and silk, a city built in the 6th century BC and rich in the past.
We went to visit gardens designed under the Qings and restored under the Mings; the classical Chinese landscape painter sought to recreate natural landscapes in miniature; the nine gardens of historic Suzhou city are exceptional and universally recognized as masterpieces of their kind.

We took a walk on "Tiger Hill" one of the historic landmarks of the Delta and Yangtze. The Tiger Hill was a temple, it was built in 961, it is forty-seven meters high. Because of its foundations, the pagoda leans.

Departure by coach for Hangzhou to the south of China at a distance of one hundred and sixty-one kilometers; Through the windows of the bus, I admired the landscapes of rice fields carved into the mountain, ethnic minorities with long hair, karst peaks forming stairs in misty landscapes that recalled old Chinese prints.... It was extraordinary !

I thought: the Chinese are doing a good job and have good ideas but during the harvest, it must not be easy to transport the rice on these rather steep slopes and there is no truck, they only do hands ; it's brave of them; hat !

We took a boat cruise on the emerald-colored West Lake, with a perimeter of fifteen kilometers and an average depth of just six feet.

On the winding road to visit a famous "tea plantation" all over China, from the bus I admired the landscapes of hills that looked like mountains, I was surprised that baboons were everywhere at liberty because, normally, they like the cold, the mists. On arrival at the tea plantation with many well aligned rows, the guide e - Tea plants are evergreen shrubs which live very well in our climates. Adults, they are hardy and can resist down to -15 ° C.
- Ah ! That's why there are no worries in the mountains.
- Are we going to see how we harvest ?

A Chinese woman showed us how to harvest tea; it is meticulous work still largely done by hand, which requires a lot of experience to obtain quality teas. Manual picking is done with bare hands, taking the bud and leaves (called the shoot) between your thumb and forefinger, and

throwing them into a hood carried by the picker on her back.
- The picking is done all day ?
- The best picking is done early in the morning.
- How many times a year do we harvest these leaves ?
- Several times a year, it grows all year round.

Departure for a very interesting visit to a typical Chinese « silk factory ». I will tell you about the manufacture of silk step by step as I have visited it, step by step. Silk is a textile fiber of animal origin. It comes from the cocoon produced by the caterpillar of the bombyx (or silkworm). The rearing of silkworms, the first step in silk making, is called sericulture.

At birth, the worm measures four millimeters. It spends the five weeks of its life engulfing mulberry leaves, reaching 10 centimeters.

The caterpillars climb on supports and are attached to them with a wire. It takes them two days to settle in and start spinning the cocoon. To form this cocoon, they regurgitate one to two kilometers of thread in four days.

First step : De-breaking
This step takes place eight to ten days after the production of the cocoon: the cocoons are re-

moved from their support and sorted. We remove the fluff or "blaze", which served to fix the cocoon.

Second step : smothering

For the manufacture of silk, the chrysalis must be killed without damaging the cocoon. The cocoons are therefore smothered in ovens at a temperature of 70 to 80 ° C, then soaked in boiling water to soften the stoneware. Sandstone, also called sericin, is a material that surrounds the silk thread.

Third step : Spinning

To find the end of each thread, the cocoons are constantly stirred with a small broom which is used to hang the first unwinding threads. In the Cévennes, this instrument was made of heather and it is made of rice straw in China.

Fourth step : Unwinding

Each thread being too fine to be used as it is, the unwinder brings together the threads of several cocoons, from four to ten depending on the size of the desired thread, and unwinds them at the same time. The wires are welded together thanks to the stoneware when it cools and are wound on "reels". The silk obtained is called "raw" silk. Finally, raw silk is itself rolled up on skeins or « floats ». It takes 8 to 10 kg of cocoons to obtain a kilo of raw silk.

Fifth step : The milling consists of twisting together several silk threads for more strength. The number of twists depends on the quality of yarn that is desired. Indeed, the more the thread is twisted, the more the fabric will be flexible. The spinner assembles the slime from 4 to 14 cocoons depending on the desired thread size (we say the "title"). The cocoons that cannot be used in spinning, the threads broken during spinning, the blazes released are gathered, washed and partially stripped of their sericin. These short filaments are then carded and combed like wool and converted into fiber yarns. The longest fibers will give the schappe, the shortest the bourrette.

Doupion : Sometimes two worms spin their cocoons too close to each other and instead of producing two separate cocoons, they will make a single double cocoon with intermingled threads. These double cocoons are spun by a special process and will provide a coarse and irregular silk thread which gives the final fabric a look highly appreciated by fashion.

Sixth step : The scouring is used to remove the sandstone by boiling the skeins in soapy water or with a solvent.

This operation can be carried out on the silk in float or on already woven silk, which then takes the name of « cooked silk ».

Seventh step : Weaving is the operation that creates the fabric by interweaving the warp threads (lengthwise) and weft threads (widthwise) on a loom. The chain is wound on a drum, the "warping machine", which allows the threads to be mounted on the loom. The weft thread is introduced between the warp threads by other processes ... compressed air, grippers, water jets.

Eighth step : Ennoblement
This is the term used to designate all of the operations that transform a newly woven or knitted fabric into a finished, ready-to-use fabric. It contains the stages of dyeing, printing and priming.

Last step : The art of the dresser is to give the fabric a desirable look and feel, without altering the intrinsic qualities of silk.

Visit of the "bonsai park" "to plant, take care of plants in a pot". These trees are miniaturized by specific pruning techniques, and by ligating their branches. They are repotted regularly in order to prune their internal roots as well as those which join the surface of the pot, in order to make an aesthetic work of art resembling trees in nature.

Cultivation is delicate, therefore the size significantly restricts the number of varieties that are likely to be worked.

Departure by train at a distance of one hundred and sixty five kilometers for Shanghai, the major international port of the Yangtze River Delta, one of the most populous cities in the world, made of contrasts and movement, astonishingly vibrant and colorful.

We visited the "lovely garden of Mandarin Yu" from the Ming period. This famous garden and its tea house are located in the center of the old town. It is full of bodies of water, pavilions and statues. We visited the Jade Buddha Temple, famous for its statue brought from Burma by the monk Huigen and carved from a single block of green jade; it houses a Buddha nearly two meters in height and an elongated Buddha four meters in length then we walk in the "Bund", the most touristic district of Shanghai.

We visited an "art and history museum", located in the heart of the city, on the People's Square; the Shanghai Museum is one of the most beautiful museums in China. Inaugurated at the end of the 90s, it is also one of the most modern in the country in terms of its design, organization and museography. More than 120,000 objects are on display there!

   At the end of the afternoon, we got back to the hotel earlier than usual, I had read what was inside: a swimming pool! I rushed into the bedroom to change, took the elevator in my robe and hit the 0 button;   downstairs I looked for the swimming pool; not finding it, I dared to ask reception in English :
- Where is the swimming pool ?
- Up.
- Sorry, upstairs ? And on what floor ?
- Eighteenth floor.
- Ah okay thank you !

   Surprised, I resumed my elevator by pressing eighteen and here I am upstairs; When I got out of the elevator, I walked right and left and finally found myself in front of the door posted « swimming pool » in English. I opened and, surprise! The pool was located well on top of the hotel and outside. So I put my towel and bathrobe near the door because I felt it was going to rain heavily, I took the plunge right away; wow! The water was hot, it was nice and calm, I felt at peace. A few minutes later, four deaf people, including two couples, arrived exclaiming :

- What a good surprise ! The pool is upstairs and outside; we looked everywhere, but you got there first.
- Lol ! I did the same as you, that's impressive; and I also looked downstairs first, then the receptionist said, 'upstairs'; I find that weird hee hee !
- Wow! Magnificent ! The water is good ?
- Too too good! Come on !

Suddenly the rain started pouring down, the four deaf people rushed to the door and I was staying in the water because I was already wet, it didn't change anything, and I said to them :
- Bah! It's not cold, we don't care about the rain that falls; come on !
- No, we wait for the rain to stop.
Too bad for you.

The rain stopped falling, the ground was already dry thanks to the heat; my three deaf friends were finally swimming with pleasure, it relaxed us. Coming out of the pool, while waiting for my swimsuit to dry, I admired the city below, walking around the pool ...

The flight time was two hours to Guilin, for a distance of one thousand five hundred and forty kilometers.

Guilin is set in a narrow plain, surrounded by fantastic rounded mountains and splendid vegetation dotted with ponds.

Guilin will be a first contact with the extraordinary landscapes that have sensitized so many great painters of the greatest dynasties.
The guide and Huguette informed us :
- In the hotel there are very specialized massages, if you want; you have to reserve for the end of the afternoon and stand in line.
When I arrived, the line was already long: I was almost the last.
- I am leaving out of curiosity, at what time is he available !
- Around six o'clock.
- OK it's noted.

The cruise on the Li River to the village of Yangshou, a small country town, did us good: calm because of the fatigue and also the heat, we admired the landscapes with imagination while looking at the varied hills and decorated.

We got to the hotel earlier than planned, so I took the opportunity to revise my resit exams for September. At six o'clock, a masseur came in and I mimed :
- Hello, massage my back please !

- Wait, I'll check. Alas no, I will massage your forehead because you have problems with your eyes.

I was disappointed and full of misunderstanding. How did he know I had trouble with my eyes? I had noticed that many told me I was over the moon or clumsy, etc. But this was worse.

Well ! I gave in, the masseur massaged my forehead for half an hour; It knocked me out and relaxed, and I thanked him.

In front of the mirror, getting ready for dinner, I jumped when I saw myself and exclaimed, "That's not true," because I had two good bumps on my forehead, like little horns; it was not pretty and I couldn't manage to hide it because my hair was so short. At table, the deaf made fun of me because of these two little horns.

We had an hour's flight to Canton, a fiery and warm city, teeming and bustling.
We visited the "Chen Family Home" or the temple of the ancestors of the Chen family, a wealthy and very powerful trading family of the time.

In the afternoon, the guide advised us :

- You absolutely have to go and see Tai-chi-chuan in the evening around six o'clock or in the morning very early around six o'clock.
- What is « Tai-chi-chuan"
- Tai-chi-chuan is a gymnastics of health, with a spiritual dimension; the Chinese do it every morning before going to work or in the evening after work.
- Or ?
- In several places, in public, I give you the map.
The same two old ladies M and T begged me :
- Can you come with us this evening at six o'clock.
- OK with pleasure.

At six o'clock, I accompanied the two people M and T, one on each side, clinging to my elbows, one carrying a flashlight to orientate herself according to the plan. We are well placed in a fairly bright place, in front of several rows of Chinese people doing Tai-chi-chuan in public; the ground was full and I could feel the vibration of a loudspeaker on which the Chinese followed the beat. It was beautiful to watch, those gentle gestures.

In the bus, the guide and Huguette called us :
- Do you remember the eel soup two weeks ag
- Yes !
- How did you find him ?
- Delicious !

- Well, that was snake soup.

The deaf got goosebumps and were shocked; except me, I laughed a lot, I suspected it was a trap. Oh ! The sacred guide, he got us well.

Visit of the city known as the "city of the goats" because of the sculpture of the Five Goats, then the Sun Yat mausoleum, a monument built in honor of Sun Yat-Sen, the first president of the Chinese Republic, inaugurated in 1929 as an extension of the District of Yuexiu in Canton; then visit Yuexiu Park and the Six Banyan Tree Pagoda, an old Buddhist temple, surmounted by a column of 5 ton bronze dating from the 14th century called the column of a thousand buddhas.

At the restaurant, I tasted the turtle soup; it tasted like snails but it pained me to see these poor innocent turtles killed!

Arriving in Hong Kong after three hours by train, we discovered this extraordinary port, teeming with boats of all nationalities and a fantastic diversity. Hong Kong is an English colony but I learned from the information that in 1997 Hong Kong will belong to China.

My God ! It will be really a big shock because China is a communist and poor country, while

Hong Kong is a very busy and free city with lots of buildings and skyscrapers; there is a big difference between china and hong kong and i was wondering how hongkong people would accept to live in a communist country?

As we sailed towards the restaurant which was in the middle of the waters, it was funny, this image of a restaurant like a boat; it floated, incredible !! On arrival at the restaurant, to get out of the boat you had to step over, without a bridge; I controlled myself so as not to fall or miss the step; it was not easy because it moved a lot; in addition the boat and the restaurant did not really stick together and the distance between the boat and the restaurant remained variable. I did it with no problem and then I helped Nicole, along with a few people; it was important to find the right time to jump, someone behind Nicole gave her the signal to jump at the right time. Phew! Nicole pulled it off without a hitch and I know she was scared of missing the jump; she was smiling with joy and above all with relief.

Decorated as in China, a huge room with lots of windows around to admire the city, the sea and the boats ...

In Hong Kong one can find more than fifty thousand shops and nearly nineteen thousand restaurants; incredible, you can find things to buy without problem; we passed a "Nike" store then another "Rebook" store then "Addidas" etc... I was careful not to spend too much because of the very strict customs and also because of the weight limit for my big bag.

I had a good idea : my shoes being almost completely worn out, I bought a new pair to put on my feet and another pair to put in my big bag; ditto for clothing.

When I returned to France, I warned my mother :
- Please mum, don't cook rice for a month!
- Why ?
- Because in China I ate it every day: noon and night, rice was too much.
- Ah! Okay.

Chapter 3

Turkey - 1992

A big meeting is preparing at Paris airport, 32 oral deaf people aged 19 to 72 years are gathered.

Arrived in Istanbul, a city in Turkey located on the Bosphorus Strait separating Europe from Asia, the Turkish guide gave us explanations about Turkey: elongated, the Republic of Turkey is a country located on the borders of the 'Asia and Europe. It has borders with Greece, Bulgaria, Georgia, Armenia, Azerbaijan, Iran, Iraq and Syria. The official language is Turkish.
- What is the capital ? asks the French guide.
- Easy, Istanbul! said a deaf person.
- Yeah, this is Istanbul! said another deaf.
- No it's not Istanbul, it's a trap, it's Ankara; as in the United States, whose capital is Washington, not New York, I pointed out.
- Very fair, the capital of Turkey is indeed Ankara, officially since October 13, 1923 confirmed the guide trick.
- What does the flag represent? I asked.

- Its flag has a very complex origin. It is first of all almost identical to the flag of the Ottoman Empire, the changes being in the shape of the moon and the number of branches of the star which go from eight to five.

We visited the Blue Mosque which was built between 1609 and 1616. To enter it we had to respect the rules: take off the shoes and have a decent outfit.

Ouch, I was dressed in shorts and a T-shirt; well, I was going to see, and I got to the front door.

Finally a Turkish guard stopped me from entering and said :
- It is forbidden to enter like this with your knees exposed.
So I pulled down my shorts to hide my knees.
- No, your elbows are also in the air !

He goes to look for clothes and he makes me put on an ugly outfit: a long blue skirt with an orange veil. I hate to dress in a skirt! I have to.
- Oh no, it's ugly! I said.
- No choice ! said the Turkish guide.
The manager of my group explains to me:
- It is the rule of the mosques, it is obligatory to put on correct clothes for the women: it is necessary to hide the arms and the legs.

- But I am not a Muslim; I am quite simply a tourist! I replied.
- We are in Turkey, we must respect.
- Ok I only put them in mosques.
- Yes it's right !

    I forced myself to put them on and the deaf laughed at me.

During the visit, Catherine begged me to help her secretly film; normally it was forbidden; so I got down on my knees, pretending to put my socks back on, while pointing her camera in the right direction to aim for what Catherine wanted. At the exit, Catherine checked the film and thanked me, it was successful, I was relieved and delighted for her.

    Then we visited the Hagia Sophia Church, which means "Holy Wisdom". It was built in the 6th century. There are many magnificent stained glass windows and a marble door; there are no obligations to respect. The Sainte Sophie church has become a museum but you can still admire its magnificent stained glass windows.

Then we went to visit the souk, "The Grand Bazaar". A Turkish guide advised us not to go for a walk alone because people often disappear, or there are attacks or attacks ... We therefore formed several small groups of 4 to 5 people. We stayed together without losing sight of each other and did some window shopping. It was very pretty to see and the Turkish salespeople knew how to seduce us to attract customers: it is their job. A salesperson even offered to have a young girl for tea behind her shop to negotiate a purchase, so I reminded the young girl that we should not separate or get out of the way. Finally she listened to me and we continued to visit the shops in the souk.

Then, we took the road to visit the "Fairy Chimneys" in Cappadocia, a region of Anatolia located in the heart of Turkey. It was very impressive to see; Here is their story: more than 10 million years ago, the region's volcanoes erupted and successive layers of lava gradually covered the surrounding valleys. Wind and water carved furrows in the volcanic rock, creating thousands of rocky cones. Some reach 40 meters high. The "Fairy Chimneys" were naturally used by men as natural shelters, pantry, attic, house ... The natural air conditioning guaranteed comfort appreciated by the inhabitants, heat in winter, coolness in summer. We entered to visit without separating, always in single file otherwise we risked getting lost because it is like in a labyrinth and it is dark there. We were very careful not to hit our heads as it is small and narrow. It was unimaginable !!!

As I could see very badly in the dark since I have Usher syndrome, it scared me and I took my courage in both hands to enter because I love to visit things even when there are risks, but I don't exaggerate too much anyway and I always find solutions to get there. I suddenly had a great idea, I suggested to a few people to hold hands in single file to reassure them and that was a good excuse for me too; at the time i didn't know about my illness, Usher syndrome, so i was hiding my fear of the dark. The person in the lead passed on the information: "watch out, walking", "watch out, head", "narrow passage" etc. Then we relayed; it went well, there were no injuries, phew !! I had succeeded in facing the dark and fulfilling my challenge.

During the visit to the pottery, the Turkish host asked for a volunteer to try to make a pot with a wheel. Excited, L., a young deaf nineteen-year-old lifts her finger and sits in front of the tower. The facilitator explains to him, with the help of a translator in LSF, how to start, with clay. The show begins, and it starts off strong because the deaf laugh like crazy when they see her caress something that moves and looks like a sausage! The young girl couldn't understand why we were laughing at her and burst into tears. One of us explained to her that it looked like a male penis, and she fled because she was embarrassed. At

the end of the show, I asked Catherine, with whom I shared the room, if she had succeeded in filming and she replied :
- No !
- Is that so !! What happened ?
- You see this guy who is sitting next to me on the bench. Unfortunately he had the hiccups and it made the bench vibrate, so the camera moved too much!
- Ah darn ! I said.

During the break, the street was deserted with only a few shops, mainly cabins and a few souks; we're doing shopping ; I saw a donkey, I was excited to get on it. So I approached the donkey to stroke it, the Turkish breeder was in front of me and the donkey between us. I then asked him:
- Can I ride this donkey?
- What? In turkish. Not understood !
Ah darn ! This breeder does not speak French; so I mime.
- Me ride a donkey ?
- Yes, nodding his head.
- Price? by making the sign « money ».

Suddenly, I give a little cry of embarrassment and mime ask the breeder to move his donkey :
- Move, get out.
- What? said the breeder in Turkish.

- Ah damn ! He didn't understand anything? Come ! Look ! I sign to show him.

    The breeder smiles at me without understanding and my Turkish guide arrives just at this moment, because he sees that I am angry, he asks me :
- What is going on ?
- Look on the ground !! Move this beast !! Hurry please !! It hurts, I say.

    My guide notices and understands, he orders the breeder to move his animal.
- Move that donkey! Look !! Her hoof is on this woman's foot !! Pay attention !

    The breeder is startled, attracts his animal with a carrot and apologizes by smiling and putting his hand on his heart.

    I asked my guide to translate into Turkish for the breeder: "Can I ride this donkey? We negotiated the price; finally we came to an agreement, I went upstairs and took a quiet little walk.

    We visited the city of Pamukkale which is 250 km from Izmir.

    There is an underground spring buried deep in the earth that pours out streams of water saturated with minerals. The bubbling waters of the springs, rich in mineralized substances, hollowed out enormous circular basins in the earth, flowing along the mountain slope, coating them with a thin layer of whitish limestone. It's a beautiful sight and I stepped in, it was hot, but be careful, it's very slippery.

At the two-star hotel, I shared the room with Catherine, who was hearing-impaired, and we were responsible for the floor. Cathy informed me that someone had knocked on our door.
A deaf man explained to me.
- There is a problem with the toilet!
- What problem ? I ask.
- Uh !!!
- Well, let's go see the toilets!

Once in the bathroom, I checked and couldn't see where the problem was. The hunt was working well!
The deaf man said to me :
- Look at her !
- Ah, toilet paper is missing!
So I went to the front desk to ask for it, and gave the room number.
I returned to my room and a few minutes later someone knocked on our door again. A freaked out 19 year old deaf girl told me
:
- The electricity went out when I plugged in the hair dryer !
- Ah damn !! Ok I'll see if I can get the power back on !

But in the end it didn't work; So I was forced to go down to the reception again and explained to the receptionist that there was a problem with the electricity in the room. I went upstairs with a Turkish electrician and walked into the room where there were three girls, but noticed that a girl was missing and asked the other two :
- Where's the other one?
- In the shower ! one of the two answers!
- Shit !!

I had to stay near the bathroom door and watch the girls as well as the electrician. The electrician checked the two girls and I whistled in protest.
The electrician continued to repair and suddenly the deaf girl came out of the shower naked. I jumped up and pushed her back into the bathroom to avoid the electrician's kinky gaze.
I slammed the door shut and the doorknob stuck in my hand because it had come loose from the door. So I broke the door handle! I said to myself "shit"! How were we both going to communicate through the door ?

I then had the idea of slipping a message under the door explaining to him to put his hand on the inside handle, while I put the outside handle back on; the electrician gave me a small nail to hang on the handle and then left the room. Phew! The

deaf girl was a little shocked and didn't understand why I had locked her up, so I explained to her :
- This Turkish gentleman was there to repair the socket and put the electricity back on.
- Oh ok !!
- It's best not to come out of the bathroom naked because you can't tell if someone is entering your room.
- Uh yes it's true !!
- You are lucky, there was no rape !! Hee hee hee
- Please ! Don't do it again !
- OK !
- Cool :-)
- Thank you !!
I left her room to go back to mine, really tired.

It was time to return to France; When we arrived at the airport, I noticed something that bothered me: there were two controllers, one on the right and one on the left; ah! I understood: on the left for women and on the right for men for religious issues. Very logically, I went to the women, unfortunately there was a conflict between the controller and me; I'll tell you what happened :
- Go right! by indicating me with his finger.
- Oh no ! I know where I am going and I am in the right place! I say in mime.

The controller looked at me up and down; since I always dress as a boy, she repeated.
- Go right! she got upset.
- No, me here, woman! I said.
I put my hand on my T-shirt so she could see my shape and show that I was a woman.
- Ah, excuse me ! Come, pass! the controller told me, staring at me confused.

The deaf laughed a lot; I used to be taken for a man.

Chapter 4

South Africa - 1994

It was a great day in my life to be able to fly to Southern Africa: Namibia, Botswana and Zimbabwe for two weeks with a group of thirty-two oral deaf practicing sign language. My parents took me to Angoulême train station to go to Paris. While waiting for my High Speed Train (TGV), my mother, worried, told me to be careful of myself, watch out for lions etc. One lady heard it all, of course, and told me that my mom really is a mother hen. I laughed and my mom shut up. There, my TGV arrived, we kissed each other hard on the cheeks and I sat down dreaming: wow! That's it, I was going on a long journey, for the first time in the southern hemisphere.

I arrived on time at Roissy Charles de Gaulle airport to go to London in England, then to Southern Africa: Namibia with a stopover; I met the head of the organization called Huguette and the group of which I knew a few people with whom I had already traveled in China and Turkey.

On leaving London for Namibia, on the big plane, I saw that the English had covered themselves well; I thought to myself that it was weird since it was summer and in Africa it was also hot since there was a desert. The flight lasted fourteen hours; so we slept the night aboard the plane.

Upon arrival in Windhoek, the capital of Namibia, I saw on a screen in the plane that they were announcing a temperature of six degrees on the ground; I told myself that it was not possible and that I would see well when I got out of the plane. Indeed, I left telling myself that it was really curdling; I was blowing and it was smoking, ouch! I was dressed in shorts! Quickly, I rushed into the airport to queue at customs, then retrieved my big bag from the conveyor belt, rummaged through it comfortably and put on warm clothes. Ouch! I had little warm clothes for two weeks, too bad I would manage.

We were in the southern hemisphere: the seasons were therefore reversed: in France it was summer and in Southern Africa it was winter.
The Namibian guide told us a little summary of the history of Namibia, and Huguette translated us into oral, and at the same time into sign language :
- Formerly known as South West Africa, German colony (1884–1915) then protectorate of South

Africa, Namibia has been an independent state since March 21, 1990.
- Ah, not long ago! did I say.

A deaf woman asked the guide :
- How many borders has Namibia ?
- There are four : to the north with Angola, to the south with the Republic of South Africa, to the east with Botswana and to the northeast with Zambia.

We took the road to admire the Namibian Desert; the altitude is on average one thousand meters and the highest point is at two thousand seven hundred meters. Landscapes stretch as far as the eye can see, empty of population or almost, where alternate lunar and semi-desert plains occupied by immense ranches, dry riverbeds, colossal dunes of red sand, blue or purple mountains erected. on the infinite horizon, desert coasts where life seems impossible.

We wanted to visit the Diamond Mines which are to the west; but we couldn't for security reasons, because of the risk of theft; the guide informed us :
- In 1908, the first diamonds were discovered in the Bay of Lüderitz.

The production is one of the most important in the world. I was disappointed that I couldn't visit;

I would have been especially curious to see how we find diamonds, how we cut them, etc. but I understood.

We went to the edge of the Atlantic Ocean where we saw seals, surprised to see some in Africa. On the bus, the Namibian guide told us that we didn't have to go or stay there for a long time, that we were free.
I didn't understand why he was saying that. The others were also asking the same question, well we would see. When I got off the bus, I thought to myself:
- Ah! I understand better! Oh damn ! It stinks, it's unpleasant to breathe in those smells, but what are those rotten smells?

I put my hand over my mouth and nose to avoid inhaling these horrible smells and walked over to the edge of the beach. I saw lots of seals, it was impressive !!
A deaf Swiss informed me:
- There are dead seals on the beach.
- What !! Or ? I do not see ! I say, because of the contrast issues.

She pointed at the dead seals and I understood better these unpleasant smells; then I got back on the bus after 15 minutes watching this show because I couldn't breathe. Ouch! My clothes

stank, my god! Luckily an older deaf woman, T, put perfume everywhere, it was a strange mixture of smells: dead people and perfume oh dear! After 10 minutes, everyone got on the bus and the guide was asked :
- Why are there so many dead seals on the beach ?
- These seals had to swim for several kilometers to be able to find fish to eat, because the fishermen had caught all the fish within a few kilometers; So these seals had to swim further and for several hours it quickly exhausted them and then they had to come back, they couldn't take it anymore, had no more energy so they died of exhaustion! the guide explained to us.
- Why couldn't the fishermen go further fishing since they have motor boats?
- It is not possible, because there are regulations on the zones to be respected according to the owner countries.
- Pff !! We are disgusted.
- Why weren't they buried, to avoid diseases and those unpleasant smells ?
- That's how it is, we let nature take its course, replied the guide.

Back at the hotel, the guide gave us an appointment to go see the Rhinoceros in a jeep.

- At three o'clock here! We formed several groups of six people. With this time, we hope to spot rhinos.
- Why hope ? said a deaf man.
- It's winter, they're going further north or east because it's not raining here, said the guide.
- Ah OK ! Well, we'll see later and we'll pray for them to come; this is exceptional for us hihi!
- White rhinos are actually gray skinned, they can run up to fifty kilometers an hour, it is dangerous to approach them, the drivers know them well; so don't worry! At three o'clock everyone was there, we formed groups and got into the roofless jeeps and wow! I was excited to see white rhinos, I prepared my camera without zoom, with film. On the way, things moved a lot because we drove on paths full of stones; ouch! It hurt everywhere; it was therefore necessary to hold in place in order to avoid knocks or false movements; it was not obvious. We admired the landscapes while trying to spot white rhinos impatiently. The driver communicated with the other drivers by radio transmitter connected to the jeep in order to be informed as soon as one of the drivers spotted footsteps, and therefore know where the rhinos were. My driver told us that we had spotted some; hop! On the way ! Quickly ! Ouch! It was jumping, moving a lot, knocking; ouch! The jeep braked, wow! Here we are near a beautiful white

rhino; I took photos, unfortunately it was too far away and we couldn't see well on the photos. One of us asked me verbally :
- - Please tell the driver to get closer because our cameras are not powerful enough, without zoom.
- Ok I'll translate into English! did I say.
- Please, is it possible to go closer to photograph better ? I translated into English to the driver.
- No! Cannot! Dangerous ! he told me.
- No, not possible ! Dangerous ! I translated to them.
- Please push him to come close! a deaf Swiss said to me.
- Please! I translated to the driver.
- OK ! But don't make too much noise! the driver told me in English.
- OK ! I replied.
- Ok, but don't make too much noise, silence and calm ok! I told them.
- Youpiiii ! Ok silence! they told me.

We got back on our way, we were too excited, but scared all the same, and we stayed calm; we were approaching a rhinoceros, we were taking pictures quickly wow !!! Awesome !! Suddenly the rhino took a step forward, the jeep ran away quickly, we were overjoyed and they thanked me very much :

- Thank you very much and very beautiful! I translated to the driver.
- Nothing! he said smiling.

Back at the hotel, the guide and Huguette came towards us, they scolded us while looking at me:
You are crazy for pushing the driver to approach this animal, it is dangerous and this rhino could kill you !
- Oh ! We made it home safe and sound, all is well! replied a deaf while protecting me.
- Ok and don't do it again !
- Ok ok !!

My group supported me and thanked me again, jumping for joy; we couldn't realize what we had done. It was madness! Obviously the other groups were disgusted but they asked us to send them some pictures later.

The guide gave us another pleasant surprise and gave us another appointment in the evening at half past five to admire lions and lionesses.

I said to myself in my head: Ouch! It is already dark, at this hour I see nothing; how am I going to spot lions in the dark? I do not understand. Well ! Never mind ! I have too much curiosity, I take risks as usual and I will see later. And no need to take my camera because it isn't powerful enough to shoot in the dark, especially since I can't see anything.

At half past five we were ready to go and admire the lions and lionesses, we formed the same groups and remained silent. I asked a deaf Swiss :
- Please can you stay near me, I can't see well at night.
- OK no worries !

I groped into the jeep, bumped into the bar at the top, without saying anything. On the way ! Oh fuck ! Full of insects; I put my hand over my mouth and nose to keep insects out, and put on my sunglasses; luckily I had taken them! A few minutes later, the headlights went out, and also the engine. Everyone had already come down except me because they had been scared and rushed to take cover and the Swiss had forgotten me! Pffff ! I was starting to panic a little as I felt the seat. I gave a little cry to let them know I was there; phew! Someone caught me saying shhh! And walked me to a security tunnel; I dabbled everywhere to understand and know where I was; I understood that I was safe in the tunnel, I was reassured and calm and sat down on a wooden bench, but I still couldn't see anything, I was a little disappointed.

A few minutes passed, the projector turned on, I said to myself: phew! Thank you for the light and I looked around to know exactly where I was: I saw wire fencing in front of me and saw a large piece of meat; a lion approached it, I was amazed to see it, then two lionesses arrived, the show began in silence, it was beautiful to see and ah thin! I didn't take my camera, too bad!

At the end of the show, I grabbed someone to go to the jeep and walked back to the hotel happy. Before going to dinner, I had to take a shower because on the way I had received lots of bugs on my hair and face; It was disgusting.

After dinner, we went to admire the moon and the twinkling stars; very close to the hotel, there were small lampposts so that suited me, unfortunately I did not see the small stars, only the big stars and I did not understand because the others told me that there were plenty of twinkling stars and it was beautiful to see. I felt something weird on the floor, like something tickling me; it made me shiver so I quickly went back to my room, and asked Catherine who I shared the room with like in China and Turkey :
- Did you smell something on the floor? I told him.
- No nothing at all !
- Is that so ! It does not matter, I dreamed! I chuckled.

The next morning, I still asked the guide, it still continued to bother me :
- Last night, I smelled something weird outside on the floor, what was it ?
- Ah you felt! They are termites! he replied.
- Ah! I have goose bumps; that reassures me, I did not dream; hi!

The guide pointed to termite nests with earth mountain shapes and a deaf one asked a question :
- What are termites ?
- Termites are white ants.
- How high are the termite mounds ?
- They can be up to six meters tall.
- It is enormous ! That's a lot of termites !
- Yes, termites produce up to thirty-six thousand eggs per day.
- Wow !! we exclaimed.

In the evening, the guide informed us that the next day we were going to visit and admire the natural national park, that the departure would therefore be at six in the morning; we would have to get out of the park at half past five in the afternoon, otherwise we would sleep in the desert on the bus. A deaf woman, V, panicked because she didn't have a vibrating alarm clock and was sleeping on her own. How to do ?

I had an idea and asked him :
- Where's your hut? What number ?
- Over there, it's number 13.
  I called everyone.
- Who is number 13's neighbor ?
- Me ! Said a deaf elderly person, M, raising a finger.
- Do you have a vibrating alarm clock ? I asked him.
- Yes I have one, but I will need it !
- Ok, please come! that we discuss together.
- OK ! the older person told me.

Deaf V, two elderly people, M and T, and I spoke to find a solution for the wake-up call. I explained to deaf V :
- This woman has a vibrating alarm clock so she takes your key; in the evening she closes your door but you don't put the lock, ok? That way in the morning she will open your door to wake you up, it's the easiest.
- **Ah good idea! they told me.**
  Phew ! The problem was solved.

At dinner, in a large, moderately bright room, on a long table, lots of different dishes were spread out, I had spaghetti bolognese, my favorite dish, especially pasta, I tasted and I found it delicious, well spiced; the guide and Huguette came to me

at my table because I was the only one who had spicy spaghetti bolognese, they asked me :
- How good were those spicy spaghetti bolognese ?
- Yes, delicious with a lot of spices; wow! I loved.
- What was that meat ?
- Well some beef! I told them.
- Oh no, it's Oryx! In Namibia there are no oxen.
- Did I notice that there were no oxen but we could have delivered meat from abroad ?
- No, that would be too expensive!
- OK ! Oryx tastes the same as beef.
- Yes almost.

Around me at the table, the deaf went to have some very spicy spaghetti bolognese to taste; they found it very spicy but delicious.

The next day I got up at a quarter past five, without an alarm clock, oh! How hard it was to get up so early, I didn't take a shower because I had taken one the day before to save time; Catherine checked the whole room and we went to have breakfast on time with our suitcases, everything was fine, everything was quiet. Suddenly two elderly ladies, M and T, approached me, getting angry :
- Hello ! What is happening ? I tell them.
- Hello. Bah! This deaf girl, V, has put the lock on, so it's impossible to wake her! What to do ?

- Oh no, that's not true! Are you sure ?
- Yes ! Go see for yourself! the elderly lady told me, T,
- Ok I'm going, come with me because I don't know where it is.
- OK ! she got upset because she hadn't had breakfast.

I looked at the time and looked up at the sky exclaiming, "My god! It's almost six in the morning, we won't be there on time! ". So we ran to the hut, I tried to open the door; Unfortunately, yes ! She had put the lock! I checked myself and told the elderly lady T :
- I'm going behind his hut, maybe the shutters are open.
- OK ! Quick and watch out for snakes!
- Yes, I said.
  A few minutes passed; I'm back.
- Its shutters are closed, shit! What to do ?
I tried to knock on the door loudly, without success, and looked at the time: my god it's six twenty in the morning.
- Ah! Twenty past six, we should have already left; you have to go and inform the guide!

The elderly lady, T, and I got to the bus; Huguette spoke to us angrily :
- Did you see the time? We are late ! Where is the deaf V ?

- Calm down ! We have nothing to do with it: deaf V has put the lock, so it's impossible to wake her; we tried to find a solution without success! I told him.
- It's not true ! Why she put the lock; yet you explained it well to him; pff, what can we do ?
- Ask the receptionist ?

The receptionist is not there, considering the time.
- Well ! Do we have to demolish the door with a crowbar that's on the bus? We do not have a choice ! did I say.
- Ouch ouch, yes we have no choice !

Huguette asked the driver to help her break the lock because the deaf woman was still sleeping; the driver, Huguette and the elderly deaf went there; I got on the bus heartbroken because they were going to break the door because of her, while we are in a poor country. A few minutes passed; at last they arrived; deaf V was shocked, disheveled, embarrassed and sat in a corner of the bus; everyone got upset because we were leaving an hour late. Huguette told us :
- Keep calm. Looking at the hour, we will be driving at high speed so we will not admire the landscape.
- Pff! All because of this deaf V and its lock! Grrrr!

On the way, we were able to admire the landscape anyway, it was not easy to photograph well, too bad.

A few hours later, I sensed something abnormal: the bus made a strange noise; so we stopped to see the problem; the driver got off and checked, then got back on the bus and ordered us to get off and stay together very close to the bus; it was dangerous to walk away because there could be ferocious beasts and pythons nearby. Everyone came down in fear; we remained welded behind the bus and saw the flat tire; two deaf people helped the driver and his son change the big tire to save time.

A deaf Swiss woman needed to empty her bladder, and so did the others. How to do ? In the middle of the desert! We exchanged between us to find a solution ; we formed a tight circle while surveying the desert; one, in the middle, urinated then we passed the relay. Finally the wheel was repaired, we got back into the bus at full speed, relieved. But we were always late.

The journey continued without stopping. The road was straight without any bends for forty-four kilometers. We watched giraffes walking amble along the road, alternately raising both legs on the same side. It was wonderful !!!

The guide and Huguette suggested that we take the opportunity to ask the guide questions about Namibia; Huguette had an idea and offered to write our questions on a piece of paper so that it would be anonymous, I wrote two questions that I put in a small cardboard and, at the end, the guide fired one paper at a time :
- Is there no river ?
- Yes, the river is called the « Zambezi ».
- What does the flag of Namibia represent ? I said.
- The flag symbol of Namibia. Red signifies the heroism of the people and their determination to build a future of equal opportunities for all. White represents peace, unity, tranquility and harmony. The blue represents the sky of Namibia and the Atlantic Ocean, the country's water resources and the precious rain. The yellow sun represents power and existence. Green symbolizes vegetation and agricultural resources.

Another question :
- Considering the length of the giraffe's neck, how does she manage to drink water?
- That's an interesting question: his neck is over 2 meters; to drink, she has to spread her legs or she will die from a problem with the blood circulation due to her long neck; it feeds on leaves and flowers that are tall.
- How tall is she? one of us asked.

- It can reach up to five meters seventy.
- How does she sleep ?
- She sleeps standing up and very little: two hours a day; it's the only animal that doesn't yawn.
- How do we know that this giraffe is female or male ?
- The horns of the female are smaller and thinner than those of the male, and also, the horns of the females are covered with a tuft of hair longer than those of the males.

The guide continued to read the questions and read :
- How are animals born ?

We jumped at this silly question while looking around to find out who wrote this question.
- Animals are born naturally; veterinarians cannot intervene because there can be very dangerous wild animals everywhere.

Another and final question.
- What is the ideal month to visit Namibia and especially to observe animals ?
- From May to October.
- Between November and April ?
- It's rain, it's very hot; so it's not pleasant.
- OK ! Thank you ! we say.

At quarter past five in the afternoon, we were still driving fast, worried we hadn't left the park yet.

Finally, we arrived at the exit of the park; unfortunately the door was already closed, we were two minutes late; the driver honked several times to signal our presence, luckily the guard was still there, he opened the door to allow us to exit. Phew !! We were safe and sound. What an adventure !! What a day !!

We flew to Botswana, a country in southern Africa which is in the center of southern Africa, with no access to the sea. We arrived at the camp where we spent two nights in a military tent; with two people per tent, it was very comfortable.

The Botswana guide explained to us about Botswana :
- Formerly, this British protectorate was called Bechuanaland. Botswana adopted its new name after independence on September 30, 1966.
- What is its capital? asked a deaf man.
- Its capital is Gaborone.
- What are its borders? asked another deaf.
- It is surrounded by South Africa to the south and south-east, Namibia to the west, Zambia to the north and Zimbabwe to the north-east.

The camp manager told me where I was going to be staying. I entered the tent, there were two folding beds in it with thick duvets. Ah ! I thought to myself, the night must be freezing because of the screen on the plane where they were marking six degrees. Ouch! It's going to be a good experience; on the other side, coming out of the tent, there were bamboo trees surrounding and separating the toilet and shower, which had no ceiling or lights. And you had to watch out for snakes, monkeys and baboons when going to the toilet and first check all around and also in the sleeping bag if there were no snakes. I hurried to urinate then went back to the tent and we got ready for dinner outside where there were some lights.

At the end of the meal, the camp manager gave us information that Huguette translated into sign language and spoken :
- Stay calm and follow me in silence; OK?
We wondered what was going on and followed those responsible. We were waiting in the dark when a spotlight came on.
- Ahhhh! A hippopotamus !!!

A hippopotamus was eating the shrubs; we admired him in silence, our mouths agape, then the spotlight went off and we returned to the table.

- Sir, is it possible that the hippopotamus crushes the tents during the night? I say to the manager.
- Yes it's possible !! But it's rare !

Ouch ! As we were deaf, it scared us. In the tent, it was starting to curdle, I dove under the thick duvet to control; there was nothing at all; too bad we would see tomorrow, and I slept soundly ...

In the morning, the smell of coffee woke me up, I saw the waiter who told me that there were hot coffees on the bedside and I thanked him. Ouch! It was curdling, I couldn't get out of my bed, I rummaged on the floor near the bed to look for my clothes, I dressed under the duvet and I told myself that the tent was still standing; phew! I woke up my neighbor by bringing her a coffee. Hop! The shower outside; hard! Hard! Because of the cold ; but, I turned on the tap to find out if there was hot water; a red water began to flow in the sink and I noticed that to go into the siphon, the direction of the swirling water was the reverse compared to France. Well, I rushed into a hot shower, then my neighbor took one too; she washed her hair then looked for an outlet for the hairdryer and asked me to help her :
- Where's the plug ?
- I don't know, maybe over there.

We searched without finding one, so: no hair dryer.

We were ready to go outside for breakfast; when we got out of the tent, we saw hippo footsteps very close to our tent; my God ! Phew !!
I ran into Huguette and asked her :
- Hello, I noticed that the water was dirty with its red color.
- No, it's not dirty, you can wash it easily, but you can't drink it.
- Why is it red ?
- There is uranium ore in the water.
- Ah ! It is not dangerous ?
- No ! It's good and it's especially for the camp.
- Ok, I get it, thank you; and also I noticed that in the siphon the water swirls in reverse to France.
- Yes that's right, because we are in the southern hemisphere.
- Ah OK !

At breakfast, the camp manager offered us three activities to choose from: either hiking, or Mokoro (an African wooden canoe), and fishing.
My choice was obvious, I chose the Mokoro and was so excited to make it. Huguette approached me and begged me to change my activity and choose fishing; I was startled saying :

- Oh no ! I refuse, I don't care about fishing, it's not my thing.
- Please change! Do it for me ! Huguette begged me.
- No !! I say without hesitation.
- Problem is, there's a deaf girl, V, all alone fishing.
- So what ! I do not see the problem ! I said.
- You know we have already had problems with it: the alarm clock, the lock etc.
- She can change activities since she is alone!
- She refuses to change, it's her passion!
- What about my passion? Why me ?
- You are the only one who can speak English and also you can defend yourself since you are very sporty !
- Well that's not fair! It's too easy ! I muttered.
- Please, I'm responsible for her, I trust you !
- Pff! I'll try to convince this girl, V, to change jobs! did I say.

I went to her to ask her to change activity, kindly, flattering her; she reacted wildly, refused with anger and Huguette begged me again and decided for me as time was ticking. I had the balls, my dream had shattered and I was disgusted. I sulked of course; I found it too unfair; the group supported me, failed to change her mind and encouraged me.

In the afternoon, the activities started, I got into a motor boat with this selfish bitch, we went for a switchback ride on the lake covered with reeds, the boat stopped, the pilot observed and m 'said in English :
- This place is not good, we are going elsewhere!
- Why ? I ask him.
- Look there ! the pilot told me in English.
- Ah ! Hippos !!

We continued our search for a great place to fish; after a few kilometers we stopped. The pilot explained to us how to fish; all of a sudden, that bitch from V got excited, impatient, gesturing :
- I can fish, I don't need someone to explain!
- Calm down ! This man is nice, he explains to us; be gentle ! I controlled myself without getting angry.
- I do not need ! I am a pro! I've been fishing for a long time, give me the fishing rod.
- OK ! Calm down ! I was really embarrassed.

The pilot was shocked but he was still smiling, I was ashamed of V's attitude and behavior; it revolted me and I said to the pilot in English so as not to break the mood too much :
- Give her the fishing rod, she can fish !
- OK ! No problem !

The pilot gave him the fishing rod and then explained to me how to hang worms on the hook ; suddenly the pilot leaned towards me saying in English:

- Stop her !!!

I didn't understand, I took my time trying to see why he said that; I spotted that the girl had tried to throw the line forcefully and I couldn't see the thread. So I stopped the girl and signed to her:
- You don't! Look, your hook got caught on the pilot's shirt on the back! Stopped ! Bah you are professional! Pff !

The girl hid, she was embarrassed. My God! The pilot asked me to remove the hook; ouch! I was afraid of damaging his shirt; I couldn't get the hook off, so the pilot took off his shirt. I checked his back to see if there were any injuries: nothing at all! Phew nothing! I was relieved and yelled at the girl because I was going crazy :
- Ah, you're professional! Bah! So here is the result! Calm down a little ok ? Apologize to him !

She refused to apologize. Oh that's not possible! What rude! I was ashamed! What a lack of respect! Fishing continued without atmosphere. Then it was time to return to camp; the pilot wanted to count the fish, I translated to the girl, who, proud of her, agreed. Paf! She had only caught six carp and I caught nine carp; she was the mouth, what character !! Pff !

Back at camp, at dinner, I recounted what had happened while fishing, everyone burst out laughing and added, laughing :
- Too bad I did not film as in video gag !
- You don't have to say that! She pouted.
- It's a joke ! Bah !
Huguette apologized and thanked me, reassured that we made it home despite the conflicts.

The flight to Zimbabwe
A bit of history on Zimbabwe: Zimbabwe has changed its name several times since its independence from the United Kingdom on November 11, 1965: first called Southern Rhodesia as a colony, it becomes Rhodesia then Zimbabwe-Rhodesia before adopting its final name on April 17, 1980. Its capital is Harare. The country is surrounded by South Africa, Botswana to the west, Mozambique to the east and Zambia to the north.

Victoria Falls is one of the most spectacular waterfalls in the world. They are located on the Zambezi River, which here forms the border between Zambia, near the town of Livingstone, and Zimbabwe. The river flows into the cataract over approximately 1,700 meters in width, and a height that can reach a maximum of 108 meters. Victoria Falls give a particularly remarkable sight, by their particular arrangement - they throw themselves into a long fault of the plateau, to escape through a narrow canyon. They can therefore only be seen from the front at a distance of only a hundred meters.

The Zimbabwean guide offered us to admire the Victoria Falls on foot and, optional for those who wished, by helicopter. First, for the hike, we were warned to be very careful because it was slippery due to splashing water and also to put on a raincoat or a k-way. We were also advised not to walk alone; so we formed small balanced groups and followed the path admiring the bubbling waters, it was splendid to see but it was impossible to take pictures because the water was splashing too hard. The few kilometers of walk went well. My appointment for the helicopter was approaching, I was too excited because it was my first baptism in a helicopter and also at the idea of seeing the falls from up there; it must have been even more beautiful to see. I went to the base with three other deaf people from the group, the organizer was doing mime to talk to us; he said :
- Hello.
- Hello.
- Well ! does he mime by wanting to say how are you ?
- Well !
- Ah I hear the helicopter coming!

- Or ? I said.
- Ah! Boom! It exploded! he said in mime.
- What! My God ! said one of us.
I was dying of laughter.
- You're crazy, it's serious! said one of us.
- But no ! He is telling jokes! Look, is there smoke? And also look at the face of the organizer! I tell them.
- Oh phew! Pff! It's not funny ! said one of us.

The organizer smiled at us and showed us the arriving helicopter and the three people asked me :
- Please go up front; we are afraid !
- OK no problem ! I say with great joy.

Oh ! I got more and more excited; the helicopter landed inside the circle, the four in the previous group descended, nauseated and relieved. It was our turn; wow! I sat in front; here I am in front of lots of dials: altitude, speed, etc ...

I fastened my seat belt and happily prepared to shoot; suddenly the pilot gave me a helmet and I said to him in English :
- I'm deaf, so I don't need to put it on !
- You put on that helmet !! he ordered me.

I had completely forgotten that the sound of the engine was preventing him from hearing me; So I put the headphones on and repeated in English:
- Hello, I'm deaf !

The pilot nevertheless continued to speak; shit, he didn't understand me; too bad I gave it up and I wasn't going to rack my brains for him; my priority was to admire the falls. The helicopter took off and flew to the falls, I was having trouble taking pictures because of the reflections of the sun on the water and also because I was a little too far away since I had no zoom; so I waved the pilot down so I could take a better shot and the pilot, who was ok, had a nice fall like bungee jumping! Wow! It was so awesome !!!

Then it was time to return to base; it had been too fast. After the helicopter landed, the organizer helped us get off and asked us :
- It's okay ?
- Yes, that was so cool! I said.
One person walked away quickly and the other two, sick, said to me :
- You're sick of asking the pilot to dive into the void; you forgot that we were behind !
- I'm sorry ! But we're alive! I sneered.
At dinner, the guide asked us if we were happy with the helicopter ride and everyone replied "Yes, but with nausea"; except me.

The next morning, we visited the Crocodile Farm; it was like at the zoo, we went all around; on the way, a man was carrying a small croco-

dile; I asked him in English while miming at the same time :
- Can I wear it ?
- Yes ! You have to hold it well because it is robust! said the gentleman while mimicking.
- OK ! I said.

Wow ! I was going to wear this little crocodile ! I asked the gentleman to take a picture of me and he nodded to say yes. It was a great day for me to be able to touch this mini crocodile. Oh that's right ! He was very robust and very restless; So I held him tight and avoided letting go or he would have bit me. After taking a picture of myself, I quickly returned the mini crocodile and thanked these men with a smile.

We continued the visit: baboons roamed freely, we paid attention and were surprised to see baboons making love, and especially to see that the female was larger than the male. You could see the red buttocks of the female baboons who were in heat, for it was rutting time.

At the hotel, at lunch, the guide advised us to taste a piece of crocodile, telling us that it was delicious !
- My god, I can't, yuck !
- Have you ever tasted it ?
- Never ever ! I said.
- It's a mixed taste of fish and chicken.
- Oh ok ! Okay, I don't mind tasting a piece of it.

- You take one of the four small pieces around the bone and you don't eat the round because it is only fat.
- OK, thanks ! I said.

At the table, I removed the fat, I tasted a small piece of it, then I finished the rest of my piece and went back to look for a few more pieces; it was really delicious.

The guide approached me :
- Ah! You took other pieces! he sneered.
- Yes, it's delicious and thank you for urging me to taste it, and especially for encouraging me; hi !

On our return to Namibia with a small plane, before going to the airport to return to France, we went to visit the Leopard and Cheetah Farm; there, a breeder showed us the difference between a leopard and a cheetah.

The cheetah is thinner, slender and can be recognized above all by its head, small compared to the body, and with two black lines marked from the eyes to the chin. The leopard, besides the fact that it most often lives in trees, is massive, less muscular and its spots are different.

The cheetah breeder offered to pet one, only the females, and one at a time. Wow! I was of course ready, the two deaf people preferred that I go first; I still got nervous when I imagined that this cheetah was going to devour me. Well ! I gave my camera to one of us and then I entered the cage with the breeder, very nice; I walked over to the cheetah and then patted it gently. Ah! It was impressive ! He purred like a cat, very sweet, I was photographed, then I walked out smiling. The two deaf people passed each in turn; it went well !

I imagined how my parents looked when I saw the pictures showing the risks I had taken by touching these animals.

Two days before returning to France, we were free to shop and wandered around Windhoek; in the evening, one of us asked :
- Who wants to go to a nightclub ?
- But we don't know if we're safe ?
- Yes, it's downstairs from the hotel.
- Is that so ! That's great ! OK !
- Meet you downstairs at eight in the evening ?
- OK ! we said.

In the evening, a few of us introduced ourselves, we chatted, danced a little, it was zen, cool. We celebrated the last day by talking to each other without realizing the time; it was already four in the morning; ouch! We had to get up at six to go shopping further out of the capital before heading to the airport. After two hours of sleep, it was hard to wake up.

At the airport, it was hard to leave Southern Africa with lots of rich memories.

When I arrived in France, I was knocked out, I took the TGV to Angoulême. When I arrived in Angoulême, my parents were waiting for me impatiently and also with concern because we did not have a cell phone to send text messages; they found me very happy and exhausted; I said to my mother :
- Here I am, look at my ten fingers, it's okay !
- Phew !

Chapter 5

South America - 1998

In February 1998, I was on university vacation and I flew with my parents to South America: Venezuela for two weeks. For my parents, it was the first time that they had traveled this far, especially outside of Europe, and had such a long flight (ten hours) !!

At the Douai station, a town where I lived in the north of France, the outside temperature was minus six degrees. The train traveled ninety kilometers an hour to the "Paris Nord" station, then we took the metro and then the RER just in service.

We landed in Caracas, the capital of Venezuela, a little late. To get to "Isla Margarita" which is located in the Caribbean Sea twenty three kilometers from Caracas, we had to go to the national airport a hundred meters away on foot. We had to collect our suitcases and go through customs. At customs, there were about 300 of us in single file for two customs officers who peeled each passport. The wait was quite long, very long; my mother was stressed because the time for our correspondence was approaching. After nearly two hours we are finally in front of the customs officer; the lady slowly checked our passports; still slowly, she finally put the seal that allowed us to enter Venezuela. During these waiting hours my parents had had time to chat with the other passengers, who were used to the country, they had advised them to be especially wary of fake taxis! You will see, this detail matters!

We quickly recovered our suitcases. Looking at the time, we realized that we would not catch the second flight. We left the international airport running towards the national airport. The outside temperature surprised us, we were sweating a lot, because there was a very big difference in temperature between France and Venezuela. It was forty degrees.

At the counter at the national airport, my mother chatted in Spanish; I have never learned this language, only English; unfortunately, the hostess told us that our flight had just left; my father was starting to get angry. We were all very tired: it had been almost twenty-four hours since we had slept, we were exhausted. My mother tried to exchange our plane tickets; at the counter, the hostess told us :

- No more seats on the next plane, I can put you on the waiting list but you don't stand a chance ! On the other hand there are places tomorrow morning !
- Oh no, it's not possible: you had to sleep in the airport or in the hotel. It wasn't our fault; It was the plane at the international airport who was late and also the customs officer who was too slow.
- Sorry, I can't do anything and come back tomorrow.

   Suddenly a Venezuelan told my mother that he had tickets to sell, for a few dollars more; my mother negotiated the price in order to get tickets that night for the plane that was to leave that night.

   I was worried because it was the first time we had been haggling and I wondered if the tickets were valid! At the scheduled time for our flight, the microphone told us in Spanish that it had been delayed. I had felt the vibrations of the microphone and I asked my mother what was being said; she answered me :
- Our flight time has been pushed back.
- Oh not possible, what's going on ?
- No idea !
- A strike ?

- I do not know.
- How long do we have to wait ?
- About two hours.
- Oh dear ! We had spent a sleepless night because of the jet lag, and it still wasn't over!
- Yes it's right.
- For the return, it will be the same, the delays between the national airport and the international airport are too short ?
- Yes.
- So it is better to change the tickets before; tomorrow morning we will go to the agency to be reassured.
- Yes, you're right.

    Finally our flight was confirmed, we went to the boarding counter, phew! Our tickets were valid; phew! We were installed on board, exhausted.

    During the trip, a neighbor of my mother chatted with her and gave her information in Spanish; then my mother explained to us :
- He told me to watch out for taxis; another one that tells us to beware.
- Why ?
- There are fake taxis.
- Is that so ! And then…
- Margarita Island is beautiful, especially the beaches, the landscapes and there are many small islands.

On arrival at Margarita Island, our luggage in hand, we exited the airport, still scorching hot. We were looking for a taxi to get to the hotel; when suddenly a Venezuelan dressed in uniform, with a cap like a guard or an American soldier, asked us if we needed a taxi.

My mom answered him in Spanish, telling him that's what we wanted. I was startled because I saw that he had whistled for a cab; that sounded weird to me. Our luggage was in the trunk and the three of us were in the back, I was between my parents and I looked at the front of the car, then I told my parents :
- This taxi is a fake.
- What! How do you know ?

I had difficulty reading my mother's lips because of the darkness and asked her to repeat me several times.
- Look, there are no meters, no cards, no handles to open from the inside.
- My God ! It is not possible ; what to do?
- Let's stay calm, I have an idea: mom, you pay when you get out of the taxi and then, dad, you get our suitcases from the trunk; as soon as you finish, i get off the taxi.
- Ah good idea. OK !

- Mom, prepare your money; You don't have to show him that you have money, you have to hide it.
- OK!

My poor parents, on their first trip so far, things were off to a bad start, I thought.

At the hotel, the driver came to take out my father who took the luggage from the trunk, my mother went out to pay the driver; as soon as they were done, I got out of the cab. Phew! Everything was fine! Our first experience with a taxi ended well. He had not taken our luggage: we had been told that they were removing the passengers and that they were running away with the luggage.

At the entrance of the hotel, a guard told us in Spanish :
- Hello and welcome to Venezuela.
- Olé, thank you.
- Alas! You took a fake taxi!
- Yes, my daughter warned us and at the airport the man whistled to call the taxi; we got screwed!
- Yes, be careful next time!
- Thank you.
- Good night, see you.
- Thank you and good evening.

At the reception, my mother presented the reservation papers, the receptionist gave us the keys. We went to the bedroom, my parents discovered that the windows did not close, since there were no handles; So my mother went down to reception to demand that our room be secured. Finally the receptionist gave us more keys, and, on the way up, my mother told us to change rooms.

In the other bedroom, the rooms were much more spacious; we installed everything, but we were exhausted.

The next morning the sun was shining and the heat was already rising. My mother asked reception where the travel agency was to change the plane tickets for our return trip between Margarita Island and Caracas; the receptionist showed us a way through the beach.

We walked along the beach; It was not very late, but the rays of the sun were already hitting hard on our shoulders and heads, as we were almost at the equator where the sun is closer to our heads than in France. Dead fish littered the thick-grained sand; it was time to get out of the beach as the receptionist had told us. At the sight of the slums, my parents were afraid and we did not feel safe; we continued the search for the travel agency with the help of a map.

At the agency, the lady took care of changing our return tickets; the problem was fixed for a small fee. It's time for lunch, I told them :
- We're going to a restaurant in the slum over there.
- What? cried my distraught mother.
- You have to try to go anyway otherwise it may take a long time to find one! I assured them.
- Uh! OK.
- If you don't like the menu, let's change !
- Ok here we go !

When we entered the brewery, a giant television was showing a football match: in Latin America football fans are numerous; there were a lot of regular customers there, the atmosphere was good so it had to be a good brasserie. A waiter offered us in Spanish :
- Hello, welcome, do you want a table ?
- Yes, for three people for lunch, please and thank you.
- Here is your table and I bring you the menu.

A few minutes later the waiter gave us menu cards. While I was reading it, my parents asked me :

- You chose ?
- Yes, I definitely have the squid and fries, which I understood in Spanish.
- Ah! U.S. too.
- You see this place is nice and cool.
- Yes phew !

   The waiter wrote down our choices and a few minutes later served us. I exclaimed when I saw the dish :
- Wow! Huge this dish !
- Yes, we can't eat all that
- Hee hee! Wow! Twelve squids! In the Canary Islands we didn't even get five for the same price.

   In the restaurant the regulars came with a box and put half of their meal in it, they took it home for the evening or for another person.

   We had a great meal and we paid. When we left the brewery, we tried to find our way to town. On the sidewalk, my parents walked in front and I followed them, it helped me not to strain my eyes too much; bang! my left leg falls into a very deep hole, luckily my right leg is holding on; I had the right instinct to avoid falling into that hole, but I lost my balance and fell forward; luckily my father was in front of me; So I pushed him and at the same time grabbed his shorts so I wouldn't fall to the ground. Phew! I was saved but my father was shocked and scolded me :

- I finally! Be careful.
- I have not seen.
    - You're still in the moon!
I didn't do it on purpose, I didn't see, but why isn't this hole protected by an iron plate?
- Given the poverty, people had to steal it to sell it.
- OK.

    I thought: Pff! I have to look everywhere without following my parents, that's better; but I don't understand why I can't see below, they can see everywhere; that revolts me.

    As we left the slum, we walked around town and noticed that at each store there were two policemen or guards or guards in uniform, armed. My parents wondered :
- Why these armed men in front of every store
- No idea, maybe thieves given the political crisis and poverty.
- Yes it is possible, one day I will ask for more information.
- It would be interesting to know more about their culture.

    Around three in the afternoon, the heat reached forty-two degrees; the air was very dry, we were thirsty; the sellers of squeezed oranges were selling fresh orange juice, we had a great time and it did us good.

In the evening, the hotel attendant called a taxi, a real one this time, to take us to the restaurant. At the end of the dinner, my mother chatted with the waiter, then she translated for us :
- I asked him about the armed police in front of the restaurant.
- So what ! I said.
- Many leave without paying because of the political crisis.
- Ah, that's why !
- Those who leave without paying, the police catch or shoot them.
- Yeah, so you have to pay ! Hi !
- Politics are going very badly now, there are violent demonstrations in Caracas.
- But now is the carnival season ?
- Yes, and some tourists got scared and took refuge in the hotel until it calmed down.
- Especially at night, is it worse ?
- Not even during the day.
- Ah darn !

For the second week, we moved; we had reserved a small villa a little further with a kitchen, and a huge swimming pool in the center of the pavilions. In this swimming pool there was a bar, in the middle, and from ten o'clock the residents were consuming all kinds of drinks and especially alcohol; the water was very hot as the heat outside reached forty-five degrees; and nearby was a volleyball net.

One morning at breakfast, my mother plugged the toaster into the first outlet, near the window, but it didn't work; So she moved it to the second take near the front door; and it worked ; then she put several pieces of baguettes of toast; a piece of wand began to smoke and suddenly the alarm went off; my parents panicked, they didn't understand what was going on; I saw the smoke rising from the toaster towards the smoke detector on the ceiling; my mother hadn't seen it, so she unplugged it right away and put it outside; but the alarm was still ringing! I laughed, and wanted to see the Venezuelan firefighters in action; but not a firefighter came; it's weird.

The weather was beautiful and still very hot, we went for a catamaran ride to an islet of white sands to walk on the beach where there were no trees, only fine white sand, my father told us :
- Put on Sunscreen cream.
- No need ! did I say.
- Yes !
- And you ?

An organizer offered us a coffee, my mother and I accepted. A few minutes later, my mother had nausea, seasickness forced her into the cabin. My dad and I sat in front, it was nice, we were splashed and we saw dolphins in the distance; it was wonderful ! On arrival on the islet of white sands, my father and I were able to get off the boat and swim to the beach, my mother did not want to because she does not know how to swim well, and she did not want to leave the bag containing our personal belongings aboard the unattended catamaran. After a while my dad and I wandered around; I noticed something abnormal: it was a little dark, I didn't understand what was going on; I then asked my father :
- Can't you see something abnormal ?
- No nothing at all.
- But yes, it's getting darker and darker.
- Oh yes it's true ! my father said after a few seconds.
- Give me your sunglasses.

I put on two pairs of sunglasses, watched the sun, and exclaimed :
- Ah, a three-quarter eclipse !!! Wow look !
- Yes, barely, it is indeed an eclipse.

When I got back from the catamaran, I asked my mother :

- Did you see the eclipse ?
- Oh no, I didn't see it, are you kidding ?
- No, ask dad.
- Ah! I missed it, I saw that it was getting darker but I didn't understand.
- Tonight, we'll watch the news on television.
- OK !

When I got back to the residence, my father took a shower and felt sunburns everywhere, even on his feet, so he spread after-sun cream; but for mum and me it was good.

On television we were shown images of the eclipse; we didn't know it before; so it was lucky to have been able to observe this very infrequent eclipse.

Still beautiful weather and still the heat. We decided to take a jeep ride with a guide to drive it. He took us to the most beautiful beach, very long, with a fishing port; on the way, we were able to observe the very arid landscapes, and, after an hour, we were on the splendid beach; my parents visited the fishing village without me because it didn't interest me; the guide therefore suggested that I walk by the sea to the point, I was up for it. I took off my shoes and screamed :
- The sand burns, impossible to walk barefoot

- The best is to soak your feet in water.
- OK !

So I ran towards the sea because the sand was so hot and then I walked in the water; It did me a lot of good, and the guide and I chatted in English at the same time as we were doing mime; we understood each other very well.
- Are you glad you came to Venezuela ?
- Yes, the landscapes are beautiful to see, especially the beaches with very clean and transparent water.
- Do you play sports ?
- Yes of course.
- I did judo.
- Ah! Me too.
- Ah ! What color of belt do you have ?
- I have the black belt and you ?
- Brown.

Our discussions continued, one moment he said to me :
- We have the same points in common; why don't we get married ?
- Ah! It's not possible, you live in Venezuela and I live in France.
- It's okay, come live with me !
- I like living in France, not here.
- Why ?

- I don't speak Spanish and our cultures are completely different.
- It's okay, you'll learn quickly.
- Uh! No sorry, we don't know each other well.
- OK I understand.

The ride lasted two hours, it was nice. We joined my parents, there was a restaurant nearby; at the table, a multicolored parrot was walking on the table and approaching me; a Venezuelan took my arm to lengthen it, and the parrot stepped on my arm; I was a little scared because of the claws; well no ! It was sweet.

When I returned from the jeep ride, I took the opportunity to swim, I soaked myself in very hot water, a Canadian offered me to play volleyball with the group in the pool, I accepted.

I had to be careful not to punch or hurt others, because I have a hard time looking at the ball, people and the net at the same time, and avoiding the sun, because of my visual field which is lower than normal.

Everything went well, a Canadian wanted to chat with me and his friends in English, also using mime :
- Where are you from ?
- Sorry, I'm deaf, and please speak quietly.
- Do you hear nothing at all ?

- Yes, that's right, that's it !
- Ok and where are you from ?
- From France and you ?
- Ah, you speak a lot of English.
- Thank you ! I say smiling.
- Me, I come from Canada, north of Vancouver and this one near Montreal !
- I see there are a lot of Canadians here ?
- Yes ninety percent in these residences.
- Ah, that's huge !
- Oh dear, my friends phoned me right now: in Canada, it's minus 40 degrees !
- Oh dear too cold !
- Yes, we're fed up, the cold lasts too long at home and we don't want to go home.
- I understand you, the difference is eighty degrees. Ouch !
- In France ?
- When I left, it was minus six degrees.
- Oh anyway, it's cold.

  Our conversations didn't last too long, but it was fun.

  At Caracas International Airport, we had problems again: we were in the queue when we were told that more tickets had been sold than seats on the plane; they therefore asked for volunteers to postpone their departure, or to go through Amsterdam. Arrival at Roissy would be delayed by two hours and we would have compensation of two hundred francs per person; we couldn't accept because my mom had an afternoon bridge competition and we couldn't afford to delay our return.

In Paris, we took the High Speed Train, the TGV. We were tired from the jet lag. In the wagon, after a few minutes, there was an announcement saying that the TGV was not stopping at the town where we were to get off; my parents did not understand why because, for two weeks, we had been cut off from the world, so we knew nothing about everything that had happened in France and in the world. My mother asked a neighbor for more information, then she informed me :
- This TGV goes directly to Lille because of the strikes.
- Oh not true! Pff! So we will take the TER to Lille.
- Yes and how are we going to tell my daughter to come and pick us up later ?
- In Lille, there is a telephone booth.
- Yes. Exact.
- OK.

Chapter 6

Martinique - 1999

During training in Paris, Betty, a deaf trainee from Martinique, suggested that I go with her to Martinique during school holidays, so two weeks in February. It made me very excited to go; it was my dream to live there; So I took the opportunity to go and explore this overseas region even though many had advised me against going there to live.

At Charles De Gaulle airport, Betty wanted to be accompanied by the disabled reception service, I told her :
- Why go to the reception for disabled people? We don't need it, we get by and it's easy to find the door
- No, I prefer to be accompanied, for safety.
- What are you afraid of ?
- To miss the plane or to take the wrong plane.
- But no, the door and seat numbers are indicated on the tickets.
- Please, no, I prefer to be accompanied.

- Ok but on the way back, we manage because there are duty-free shops, we could take advantage of them.
- We'll see.

In the plane, at the entrance, there were newspapers to choose from, and free; I took advantage of it, so I took « The Team » and sat by the window; well I was going to be able to admire Paris because we were leaving in the middle of the afternoon, when it was usually night. For a moment the plane was going at high speed, suddenly Betty took my hand and squeezed it, crossing my fingers; I almost screamed because she had hurt me so much, she almost broke my wrist and fingers; at the same time I was shocked; I checked myself and put my journal on our hands because I was ashamed.

When the plane was in the air and stable, Betty finally let go of my hand, I relaxed my fingers and my wrist, saying :
- I'm not fine !! I am shocked and you hurt m
- Sorry !!!
- Uh! Are you afraid of the plane?
- Yes, a lot.
- Why didn't you tell me ?
- I was afraid you would refuse to come with me.
- I'm not like that, it's important to inform myself beforehand so as not to be surprised.

- Sorry !
- What are you afraid of ?
- Whether the plane misses take-off or explodes.
- Oh ! You watch too much news or hi movies! It's not every day.
- Yes I know.
- Then what else ?
- That's all.
   - Yes !

During the trip, Betty chatted a lot as she needed reassurance that everything was going well during the flight, so it was impossible to sleep. Soon the plane began to land, I reached out my hand to reassure Betty; she still squeezed my hand, but not as hard as she initially did.

On leaving Fort-de-France airport, it was very hot and muggy, her parents took us to "Trois Rivières", the French hamlet in the town of Sainte-Luce where Betty's parents live, j I admired the landscapes especially the beaches and the sea.

To visit the island, Betty's parents couldn't drive us, except on weekends, because of their jobs; I suggested to Betty :
- We will rent a car so we can visit freely.
- No, my parents refuse.
- Why ? I have my driver's license and I'll pay for the rental.
- My parents always refuse.

- I do not understand why ? We are adults and free.
- Yes I know, but it is better not.
- Explain me why ?
- My parents don't want me to drive because of my deafness.
- What! But I have my driver's license.
- Please stop, I don't want to have any problems.
- I'm disapointed !!!
- Sorry.

Deep down I was saying to myself: my god, what am I going to do for two weeks pff ! I don't see where the problem is and I see that Betty is submissive; poor of her! And I'm stuck; well, I'll drop it, so we'll only be visiting for about four days....

At Fort-de-France beach, strolling along the seaside, I was shocked to see lots of syringes left on the sand, and I said to Betty :
- Have you seen those syringes ?
- Yes we still find them here.
- Are these drug addicts meeting here ?
- I think so.
- But it's dangerous, it can transmit AIDS.
- Oh well how ?
- There is blood on the needles, we don't know who has the A.I.D.A, and if children see it and touch it or bite it, it's screwed.

- Oh yes it's true.
- Even us, if we walk on it with bare feet, bang ! You see ?
- Yes, very fair.
- It would be better to add a trash can there. Oh my God ! I have never seen this.

At the Salines beach, a long strip of white sand bordered by coconut palms, very frequented in Saint Anne, the water was too good and transparent: I could see my feet and sometimes fish; it was impressive.

When I got out of the swim, I felt something strange on my skin, it was itchy, it was painful and unpleasant, I didn't know why, maybe there was too much salt in the water? Betty asked me :
- It's okay ?
- Yes, but it itches everywhere.
- Is that so ! Are you allergic ?
- No never.This is weird.
- Are there animals in the sea ?
- Uh! I do not know.
- And you, it does not itch ?
- No, but a little bit anyway.
- Ok, so you better take a shower.
After my shower, my skin was soft again, phew !

In the evening, when I was going to bed, I stretched out under the sheet, suddenly I was startled because I had felt something move under the sheet; I immediately got out of bed in a panic and then lifted the sheet to see what it was. Ah! It was so cute, a green frog, phew! I grabbed it and kicked it out then rechecked under the sheet and under the bed, there was nothing.

The next morning, at eight o'clock we were on the balcony, I was telling Betty the story of the green frog, she burst out laughing; suddenly I felt a loud, sudden, brief noise, I asked Betty :
- What is happening ? I felt like a big boom.
- Yes me too.
A girl came to see us asking :
- It's okay ?
- Yes what was that noise? I asked.
- It was an earthquake.
- Is that so ! This noise was weird.
- The large table moved and then snapped back into place in ten seconds.
- Ah! Does it often happen here ?
- Yeah, we're used to it.
- This is the first time that I have felt one; I have had it in France before, but at night while I was sleeping; So I hadn't felt anything.

I said to myself: yeah the earth trembles a lot here, it scares you all the same; the table has moved, so do not leave fragile things lying around on the table or on the furniture. Ah, I understand better: I noticed that a lot of glass cabinets are closed! I see they are used to it.

I admired Le Rocher du Diamant which is a small uninhabited island located in the Caribbean Sea in the southwest of Martinique, about two kilometers from Pointe du Diamant, in the Saint Lucia Canal.

On carnival night, Betty wanted to go to a friend's house, but outside on the patio, I was like "ouch I hate the dark"; I took my courage in both hands to say to Betty :
- Uh! I can't see well in the dark.
- No worries, I'll be near you, ok.
- Uh ! OK.

I was still scared because, besides, I didn't know anyone. Night fell, her mother took us to a friend's house; getting out of the car I couldn't see Betty or her mother because of their dark skin, it scared me, I really wondered where I was.

Phew ! Betty grabbed me and led me to a shelter with a light and a table with benches. Betty introduced me to her friends and then I nailed myself to the bench to avoid being awkward when moving around. A guy called me asking :
- Hello ! Do you accept that I offer you a drink
- No thanks.
- Come on.
- No thank you, I don't drink alcohol.
- Ah OK ! And do you want to dance with me?
- No thanks, I suck.

- I'll teach you.
- No thanks.

A friend of Betty's intervened :
- Hey ! You know she's my darling; leave her alone !
- Ah, excuse me! OK.

The guy left, I thanked Betty's friend adding that it was clear that I was not his sweetheart; everyone burst out laughing.

When I got back to France, at the airport, I said to Betty :
- You promised me not to be accompanied by the service for the disabled.
- Yes, but my father wants me to be accompanied.
- Ok, that's not true! Okay, I'll leave you and I'll go on my own !
- No, I beg you to stay close to me.
- You promised me.
- OK ! I will convince my father.

A few minutes later, Betty replied :
- It's okay, my father agrees.
- Great ! We're going to be able to do some shopping.
- OK !

From the waiting room, I noticed that all the stores were closed; I had the balls, everything was wrong. After a few minutes Betty called me :
- Where's the boarding gate ?

- It's written on the plane ticket or it shows on the screen.
- Ah, I found it and where is it ?
- We have time, cool!
- No, please, we're going to the boarding gate.
- My God ! Are you scarred ?
- Yes, I don't want to miss the plane.
- No, we still have an hour to wait.
- Please !!
- Ok, let's go.
- Thank you.

Outside the departure gate, Betty begged me:
- Are you sure !
- Yeah, trust me !
- I don't smell, this's the wrong gate.
- Oh, you don't trust me; look at the plane name on the screen and the plane ticket !
- Ah it is written the same, phew thank you.

In my thoughts I said to myself: my god, Betty is really anxious and fearful; luckily I keep my cool otherwise I could have gone wild; she might crack; I pay attention to her; still, despite everything, she is kind to have invited me.

Chapter 7

Burundi - 2001

In February 2001, a week before I flew to Burundi, I finally got the visa stamped on my passport. It took a long time because of the political crisis and the civil war. I joined my Burundian friend whose name is Claudia; I knew her on the internet, we spoke by email for a year; she invited me to come and discover her country; I warned her that I am deaf Usher, giving her explanations; it didn't seem to bother her. So I took the risk of going there: it is my passion to travel everywhere and especially to discover different cultures.

At the airport, at Roissy Terminal three, after checking in my bag, I had three tickets because of the two stopovers, and spent a whole day on the plane and at the airport because there was no had no direct plane. At the first stopover, in Amsterdam the capital of the Netherlands or Holland, to change planes, I had hoped to find my way easily. I was surprised that Amsterdam Airport was well suited for all disabilities: for example, there were illuminated signs in yellow

with writing in large bold characters; the paths are very wide, so small cars as for golf can circulate to accompany people who have difficulty moving; in France, nothing is suitable. While I was looking for my way, a lady spoke to me in Dutch or another language, while tapping me on the shoulder :
- Warning !
- Sorry, I'm deaf and I didn't understand! I said in English and mimicking at the same time.

This lady showed me her finger to tell me to look behind; I turned around and saw that I was blocking a mini car from passing; I raised my right hand in the air saying "Excuse me!" I'm deaf " ; the driver calmed down, smiling at me.

A few minutes later, I easily found the plane to Nairobi, the capital of Kenya, I felt reassured. The flight lasted eight and a half hours.

On the plane, I sat near the window; a young girl with black skin, my seat neighbor, spoke to me without my noticing; for a few seconds, I was looking everywhere out of curiosity and suddenly I realized that this girl was talking to me; so I answered her immediately in English :
- Excuse me ! I am deaf, you can repeat me!
- Hello, ah okay, can't you hear anything at all? she said in English.
- Nothing at all ! I say in English.
- Where are you from ? she still says in English.

- From France and you? I say in English.
- Ah, you are French and I come from Belgium! she said in French.
- Ah, you speak French! And I burst out laughing.
- Yes hee hee, we can not know in which language to speak ? What is your name ?
- We can talk to each other on familiar terms; my name is Sandrine and you ?
- I didn't understand, can you spell me in the alphabet in signs ?
- S A N D R I N E! I'm surprised she knows the sign alphabet.
- Ah ok and me S O L E G E N.
- Where are you going ?
- In Kenya and you ?
- In Burundi.
- Wow, is your family over there ?
- No, a friend with whom I connected by email.
- Wow that's great! Is this your first time ?
- Yes and you ?
- No, my family is there, I'm going for my sister's wedding.
- Awesome.

Our conversations lasted two hours or more, I didn't see the time go by.

On arrival in Nairobi, we said goodbye and have a safe journey; I was looking for the flight to Bujumbura; here I am in front of the table at the

top; unfortunately, it didn't display anything; I felt the vibrations of a speaker; ouch! They were making an oral announcement. How to deal with my deafness? I saw a lady in her 50s or over, I spoke to her in English :
- Hello, excuse me, do you speak French or English ?
- Hello, in French.
- Oh great, I'm deaf and the board shows nothing; there was therefore an announcement at the microphone.
- Oh yes, it's true and where are you going?
- In Bujumbura.
- Oh that's good, me too.
- It's funny !
- Ok stay next to me, I'll warn you, can we go together?
- OK no problem ! Thank you.
- Are you going to Burundi for the first time ?
- Yes and you ?
- No, this is the third time because my son works in a village in Burundi, he got married and had a son recently.
- Congratulations, you are a grandmother !
- Thank you, are you going to Burundi for work or vacation ?
- On vacation with a friend.
- Do you know your friend ?
- No, we connected by email via the internet.
- Watch out !

- Why ?
- There, the political crisis is still serious and I'm a little afraid to go; but my priority is to see my grandson.
- Ah ok thank you for this information.
- I will give you my mobile number and my email address if you ever have a problem, contact me; OK ?
- Ok thank you and I'll give you mine too.
- Your first name is Sandrine and mine is Michèle.

We gave each other our coordinates. I needed to go to the bathroom, I informed her I was going to the bathroom and coming back.

In the bathroom, I saw on the left for the men and on the right for the women, so I went to the right; Suddenly the cleaning lady stopped me from entering and showed me her finger and said to go to the left, I replied by miming without speaking because of the fatigue :
- No, I know where I'm going.
- No to the left! She looked me up and down, finding me weird.
- No, I am a woman.
- No to the left.

Finally, I put my hands on my T-shirt to show her I had boobs and she apologized, still finding me weird.

I am used to being taken for a man because of my shoulders which are so broad from exercise and also because of my face which looks like that of a young man. But OK !

The loudspeakers vibrated, Michele informed me that our flight was there. As I sat on the seat, I thought about my conversation with Michèle:
« Things are going very badly in Burundi »; it's weird, my friend Claudia reassured me, that everything was calm politically and that there was no problem for me to come; well we'll see.
Through the window, I could admire Nairobi.
Oh ! There are too many buildings, hotels, it is a tourist site; It's a shame and it's ugly.

In Bujumbura, at the exit of the airport, I saw no one except a few individuals; Michèle found her son with his wife and grandson; she watched me to see if anyone was coming to pick me up; it was nice of her. At one point ten women arrived with roses welcoming me.

Ouch! Which one is Claudia because I must have found it hard to tell their black faces apart, but I know Claudia is tall; phew! Of the ten, only one is larger.

I approached her telling her she was Claudia, she smiled at me nodding her head yes; phew!

The welcome was very warm! I am not used to giving me roses. I told Michèle that everything was fine, wished her a good stay and said see you soon.

Claudia told me :
- Here it is cold, it is around twenty-five degre
- For me, it's not cold, I'm hot.
- No, it's the winter period and the summer period is rainy and very hot, over thirty degrees.
- In France, in winter, the temperature is below zero in the North and in summer around thirty degrees in the South-West.
- Ah! There is too much difference.

While taking a mini bus, the driver and the ten girls started chatting without my knowing what was going on and Claudia told me :
- Go up. Its good.
- What is happening ?
- The driver wouldn't let you get on because you're white but we don't agree, don't worry.
- Ok, here is there a problem with the skin colors ?

I dare not say the word "racist", I be careful.
- Uh! I think yes, this is the first time that I have welcomed a white woman, that does not bother me.

The road had no tarmac, it was a track: when it's dry, it makes clouds of dust, I saw real African life because there are no hotels or chic shops.... Few whites live there.

We stopped in front of a large gate at the entrance of a beautiful house; I was surprised, I didn't understand; Claudia informed me :
- This house was loaned to me by a white Belgian friend who is a pilot; so he is away for a few weeks.
- Wow! How generous this pilot is !
- Yes he is great and nice; I make you visit.
- Ok I follow you.
- Here is the kitchen,... your room...

Ah ! There are no windows at all, only mosquito nets, even in the shower, in my room. Ouch! Could it be broken into ?

At lunch, with the ten very pipelette girls, lots of various dishes were laid out on the table: there was nothing more to choose from; we helped ourselves and ate.

It seemed abnormal to me considering the poverty; this pilot may have offered him meals; if so, it is truly generous of him.

In the evening, finally, Claudia and I found ourselves alone, I had difficulty reading her lips because of the dim light and also her black skin, not easy to see in the dark for lack of contrast. I was surprised that Claudia knew the sign alphabet, but I still had difficulty seeing; so I went to get a notebook and a pen so that we could communicate in writing.

In the morning, I had slept well, I went to the kitchen, and I was startled because there was a man, I wondered who it was? Claudia then arrived and introduced him to me :
- Here is a servant who does everything, he cooks, watches over the house, gardens, etc.
- Oh okay, hello !
- Hello ! he said; and then he ran away.
- Is he afraid of me ?
- No, it's customary, he shouldn't be there when a white person is in that room except when we ring him.
- Oh the custom is strict !
- Yes and you in France ?
- At home, I don't have a servant, I take care of everything.
- Ah Super !
- I don't like to treat someone like a slave.
- Here it allows them to earn their bread.
- Yes, but it's not like that anyway: in France, among the rich, there are sometimes servants, but no slaves, I don't know.
- Ok, this week, I present to you my mother, my sisters and my brothers.
- Ok, with pleasure and where did you learn the sign alphabet ?

- At school, all the pupils were given information about the various disabilities.
- Wow ! It's really very interesting and great to learn when you are young.
- In France ?
- No nothing at all.
- Too bad, it's very human here, we help each other in case of problems.
- I saw that because all ten of you have helped me a lot, wow !
- Normal! she smiles at me.
- Thank you for inviting me and it is above all a good discovery !
- Do you need to change some money?
- Yeah, we're going to the bank to get some money from the ATM.
- What is a distributor ?
- I put my credit card in the ATM to withdraw money; it's automatic.
- I don't know, it doesn't exist !
- Ah darn ! Uh! I have money in my pocket; so can we trade it ?
- Yes to the market.
- What at the market?
- We negotiate with businessmen in the street.
- It's dangerous !
- No, my two friends are helping us change the money and you stay with me and let my two friends do it. OK ?
- OK.

At the bank, not finding an ATM for bank cards, we went to the reception, a lady asked us :
- What do you want ?
- She wants to withdraw money with a visa bank card.
- Sorry, there is no ATM but I'll see with the chef if I can do something with this bank card.
- Here's the bank card.
A few minutes later, a lady arrived telling us :
- Sorry, that's not possible.
- Why ?
- This bank card has no money.
- Sorry ? But no, there is a lot of money in it.
- I can not do anything.

It was rubbish, I was sure she didn't know about this bank card, so she found a nice excuse. Pff! I thought in my head.

We then went to the market to negotiate the exchange of tickets; in the street in town, in a corner, two men were holding banknotes in their hands without any embarrassment; the two friends approached the two men to haggle, ten minutes passed and the two girls gave me Burundian Francs; I thanked them. We walked around town, we went to the cyber café for the girls to surf the internet; I didn't want to because of the pirates and also because there was no security: everyone was walking by and could see.

Wifi rowed since ADSL was very weak but it was better than nothing.

On the road, often military trucks passed in circles; I was told that the political crisis was underway; I would have liked to know more; So I dared to ask Claudia :
- What's wrong with politics?
- Here there is a problem of religion and also with the tribes.
- In Burundi, which religion is the majority?
- Ninety-five percent are Catholic and five percent Muslim.
- And what are the tribes ?
- The Tutsis, the Twa and the Hutus.
- What are the differences ?
- Language differences between Rwanda and Burundi and especially the tension between these two countries and also with Congo.

We had a visit from Claudia's sister, with her nephews, small and cute; One of his nephews touched my hair and face and hugged me on the couch: it was the first time he had touched a white man; he was adorable. Then we went to see Claudia's mother.

At the large lake, there is Congo on the right and Rwanda on the left; we went for a walk in the sun; it was nice and I offered them :
- We are taking a shower ?

- No, that's too dangerous.
- What? I do not see what the danger is ?
- The giant six-meter crocodile is bathing there.
- What, are you kidding ?
- No it is true !
- So I moved away from the beach because I couldn't see well and didn't want to be eaten.

One of the ten girls invited me to her home, to her apartment on the top floor of a three-story building; there was still no window. At dinner, a girl passed by with a basin, I had guessed it was to wash her hands; then, on the table, there were only plates, and two dishes had been brought: one of rice and one with ground beef with tomato sauce; I was asked to serve myself first.

Uh ! How do you eat without a fork or knife? I felt stuck and embarrassed.

- Go yourselves! By finding a good excuse for me.
- Ah ! You don't know how we eat !
- Ah darn ! They are not stupid hihi !
- Exactly, show me please !

We eat with our fingers: we first take a small handful of rice with our fingertips and dip it in the tomato sauce, then presto! In the mouth !

When I ate everyone burst out laughing; I asked them :
- What is happening ?

- With each bite, you lick your fingers, it's pointless.
- Ah! Ah! It's true hi !

Two weeks had already passed, I went through customs again, a soldier checked my passport looking at me for several minutes then he went to another room next door.

Oh ! My passport ! Pity ! Don't steal it! I have to stay calm without smiling !

More than five minutes passed, the soldier came back and gave me my passport back; with a rather strict face that scared me, he ordered me to go to the waiting room; we are not laughing!

Around half past eleven, I flew to France with two stopovers as on the way there.

At home, I emailed Claudia to thank her for her very warm welcome, but after three weeks I still had no response; I was worried. I then remembered that Claudia had told me about the site of a Burundian newspaper; So I found information there: I came across an article announcing that there had been an explosion at the airport and that there had been a lot of blood on the road, so that the civil war had started again two hours after my plane took off.

How lucky I had been !!!

I sent Michele an email to reassure her and tell her that I was back home and she answered me.

Three months later, Claudia finally answered me by telling me that I had been lucky to leave in the morning because in the afternoon there had been a lot of deaths, three thousand, that it was awful and that she was well but had been scared.

Phew ! She was very much alive despite everything. We always kept in touch.

Chapter 8

Morocco - 2002

Before flying to Morocco, my hearing friend Céline and I did a lot of preparation: we read the backpacker's guide to know as much as possible about the culture, the currency ... I asked Céline in sign language :
- You have a passport ?
- No.
- But to go to Morocco, you need one.
- No, you can use your identity card or passport, it's written in the backpacker's guide.
- Ah Super ! And please check if the date has not expired ?
- OK ! ... Its good ; two more years.
- Phew! Everything is fine.
- If the date has expired, what happens ?
- We refuse to leave France.
- Is that so !
- Yeah, customs are strict.

It was Celine's first plane trip. At the airport near Bordeaux, Céline and I collected the papers from the counter marked Fram, the hostess asked us :

- Please, your passports or ID cards.
- Here !
- Here are your papers, you go to the registration to get your tickets with the seat numbers, and to register your luggage; if they are less than 2 kilograms, you can keep them with you; don't lose your passports or identity cards and have a good trip.
- Thank you and where is the recording? Celine said.
- Right, then straight ahead and you will see the number on the screen; then you go to recording.
- Ok thank you and goodbye.

    For a while, we checked the papers; Celine tells me in sign language :
- There is a problem for these two women.
- Oh, what is it ?
- Her identity card has expired so she does not have the right to leave France.
- Yes ouch! She will lose her trip.
- You see !
- Yes.
- But a woman tries to telephone the prefecture to try to find an arrangement and obtain a temporary paper.
- What do you mean ?
- No idea !

- Too bad for them, it's not our problem.
- Right, it's true; we go to the recording !
- Yes and how are you? Aren't you nervous for your first flight ?
- No, it's okay because you're here with me.
- Ok cool, here we go.

At check-in, our luggage is walking on the conveyor belt; we have the tickets, one of which is near a window, and at customs, someone checks my passport and Celine's identity card; then we go to the waiting room, and we both discuss :
- Oh dear, we had to show your passport and my identity card several times, it's really strict! Celine told me.
- Yes, it's because of migrants, political asylum etc ... It's the law.
- Oops! Ah! It's over to us, let's go.
- We will again show my passport and your identity card with our tickets; so get ready.
- What! Again !
- Yes hee hee !

On arrival in Marrakech, Céline and I were afraid because we had the impression that the pilots did not know how to fly because, for the landing, the plane descended too suddenly, swayed to the right and to the left and landed abruptly on the runway.

Marrakech is a city located in the south of Morocco, in the interior, at the foot of the Atlas Mountains.

In the evening, to let off steam after 4 hours of flight, we went for a walk and visited the souks; we followed the plan drawn by the hotel receptionist; on the way there were shops, we were surprised to see meats invaded by flies: it is a lack of hygiene, but given the poverty it is impossible to have refrigerators; we continued to the souk, it was a huge place with lots of souks, what a crowd! My friend and I stayed glued to each other to avoid getting lost and especially since I couldn't see anything at night; suddenly Celine scolds me in sign language :
- Why are you pinching my butt ?
- What? It's not me ! I jumped.

I looked around, saw a few guys behind us, pff ! Draggers !!
- Ah ! These are the guys who pinched you, hee ! Because you are beautiful, especially blonde and you have beautiful blue eyes! But still it is not done! I said.
- Pff, why not you ?
- Normal, they thought I was a guy, that's why!
- What luck pff! And that pisses me off ! In addition, they hit on me with words !

- Ah darn !! Phew! I am deaf and very quiet !
- Yeah! Grrr !
- Well, I stay in front of you to protect you, so that they will leave you alone. OK ? I said.
- OK !! Thank you !

We continued the visit then took the road back to the hotel; it was already exhausting us because the Moroccans were constantly flirting with us, it was incredible! And besides, we were surprised to see the guys walking around hand in hand or on each other's arms like lovers. I said to my friend :
- Are they gay ?
- I also wonder !
- But do you see women ?
- No, only men !
- Ah! Is this their culture? I said.
- We will read the backpacker to better understand their culture !
- I know that women must always stay behind men, it is their religion! I said.
- Ah OK !
- Yes, we're going back to the hotel !

In the bedroom, we read the backpacker's book; unfortunately they didn't talk about it, too bad !

The next morning, we returned to the Place des Souks because I knew I would see more clearly

than the night before; my friend informed me in sign language :
- There is a snake!
- Ah! Or ?
- Over there !
- I can not see ! Show me please !
- Ok come on !

I followed her under the souk, a Moroccan was playing the flute; opposite, a wicker pot; inside, a cobra was dancing on the way up, impressive !! Suddenly Celine ran away like a rocket, I couldn't understand and looked around. Ah! A Moroccan was next to me and smiled at me, I also smiled out of politeness, but why Celine had gone like a rocket? The Moroccan showed me my camera, that meant he wanted me to photograph it, I said politely no to him because I knew that if I photographed a person, I had to tip him; I refused, and besides, he was not handsome. I joined Celine and asked her :
- Why did you run away like that leaving me ?
- Ah ! Haven't you seen anything ?
- See what ?
- The Moroccan wears a snake around his neck !
- Is that so ! I have not seen ; wait for me, I'm going back there to have a good look; OK ?
- Be careful !
- Do not worry !

I went back and approached, oh yeah! This man did have a real snake around his neck. Luckily I have Usher Syndrome hihihihi !
I joined Celine by signing her from afar :
- It is true ! Thank you for telling me !
- Didn't you notice anything ?
- No, because my visual field is weak; i'm lucky i couldn't have been afraid hihi !
- Pff ! Yeah !
- We will see over there, I think there is an underground souks; inside there are magnificent shops; I saw it in the backpacker's guide.
- Ah yes just ! Let's go !
- Yes !

We went inside, it was dark, I held Celine's elbow to guide me so I wouldn't do any awkwardness: spilling things, breaking nice dishes etc ...

We admired a lot of things, it was wonderful! I stopped in front of typical Moroccan lamps with several colors, I approached to see better while taking my time, suddenly a salesman hugged me and hugged me; I was shocked and almost pushed him hard; luckily Celine told me shhh! And please calm down. I checked myself without understanding, the seller apologized by putting his hand on his heart and leaning over; I was embarrassed, I didn't understand, it annoyed me and I didn't like it.

Finally Celine told me in sign language :
- When you admired the lamp, the seller said to you: "Hello and welcome to Morocco", but you did not answer him; he kept talking to you, still without an answer from you, as if you didn't care; then his tone went up, I heard his voice louder, so I told him that you were deep deaf; so the salesperson was ashamed and took pity on you, so he hugged you to apologize !
- Ah ! That's why ! But still in the arms, it is not done! Oh damn I was shocked !
- It is true ! I didn't think he was going to do this ! Hi !
- I thought he was going to rape me! Hee hee !

We laugh, oh there! Now I have to move my head to look around me.

In the evening, we went back there again; I suggested to Celine :
- Handmade orange juice? Too delicious, come on !
- OK !

Suddenly a veiled Moroccan grabbed me with joy, waved at me but I couldn't understand a thing because it was dark and she was also veiled, so I couldn't see the expression on her face; I asked

Celine if she understood; well no ! Ouch! I was stuck, so I dared to ask her mimicking :
- Please, can you take off your veil?
- No, that's not possible !
- I need to read the facial expressions with the signs !
- Here it is forbidden to remove the veil !
- I know, but the problem is I can't see well.
- Ah OK ! I don't lower it for long ok ?
- OK, thanks !

The deaf Moroccan took off her veil and repeated; ouch! I still did not understand because she was speaking badly and I asked her to put on her veil out of respect. Suddenly a deaf Moroccan joined us and helped me by translating into international sign language; phew! Saved by the Bell! So we exchanged :
- She has never been to school so she signs as with a family code.
- Ah OK ! I get it.
- Excuse me ! I have to go, but can we meet tomorrow afternoon at the bar over there ?
- Wait, I'm discussing it with my friend.
- Why not ! Celine told me.
- Ok it works and see you tomorrow around 2pm! I said.
- Great ! Thank you ! See you tomorrow ! he said.

Céline and I were happy to meet deaf Moroccans; it was nice.

In the afternoon, our meeting took place, the deaf Moroccan came with a friend, so there were four of us; it was cool, we talked about Moroccan culture.
- Uh ! Do I notice that there are a lot of gays here ? I ask them.
- No, they're like that, they're like friends.
- Ah OK ! Because in France, it's homosexuals.
- Yes I know, my brother lives in Finland, I learned that: each country has a different culture !
- Yes it's right ! It's important to respect! I said.
- In Morocco, how many schools for the deaf are there? I said.
- Only one, in Rabat !
- Ah, that's not much! said my friend.
- Yes it's a financial problem, it's too expensive ! Yesterday evening you met this deaf girl.
- Yes I remember.
- She never went to school, her parents hid her because they were ashamed, as a punishment from Allah, no one knew they had a deaf daughter !
- Ah darn ! Now is that much better? I said.
- Yes, thanks to King Mohamed 5 !
- Alcohol is prohibited, but you drink beers?
- Hi ! That's right, the law evolved thanks to the king; we are more flexible than Algeria, Egypt.

- Ah ! I understand better. And what are the most attractive tours you can find around Marrakech?
- Essaouira and Ouarzazate ... and further afield, Fez, Rabat and Casablanca. He said.
- What are we visiting in Essaouira? I ask them.
- Essaouira is located at the edge of the Atlantic Ocean and we visit the port, the fort; before the Portuguese invaded it and then abandoned it and it's beautiful to see !
- And Ouarzazate ?
- Ouarzazate is a city in southern Morocco. It is nicknamed « the door of the desert ». And also there are sites where films have been shot; do you know the movie Lawrence of Arabia ?
- Yes I saw this movie, I love it.
- This is where this film was shot in 1962 on the site of Aït-Ben-Haddou, a small village near Ouarzazate.
- Is that so ! I did not know !
- You have to go there absolutely, especially by jeep! he tells us.
- OK, thanks ! we say.

The exchanges lasted 4 hours, it was very interesting and fun, we had to leave them because we had dinner at the hotel.

We visited the palace of Marrakech, we walked around it, it was beautiful to see, we could see storks, then we went to the bus station to book 2 bus tickets for Essaouira.

We stood in line in front of the counter, Celine asked the clerk :
- Hello, 2 tickets for Essaouira for tomorrow please ?
- What? he pronounces in Arabic.
- Ah darn ! Celine told me.
- What is happening ?
- He can't speak French.
- Ouch! Hold on !

I write: "Essaouira", then I mime: « 2 tickets, tomorrow, not today »
- OK ! said the clerk.

The clerk writes: 5 am then he mimes : « leave »
- Ok and back? I mimicked.
- Not here, there buy.
- Is that so ! Ouch! We don't know in advance for the return trip, I say to Celine.
- Too bad, we go there anyway and we will buy 2 tickets in Essaouira, long live the adventure !
- OK no problem !
- Ok buy 2! I mimicked the clerk.

We exited the bus station towards the hotel while discussing :

- We take risks by not taking the return! If we don't have return tickets, we'll have to find a night at the hotel! Celine told me.
- Yes ! We won't have a choice and you're sorry ?
- Uh no ! But I'm a little scared.
- It's adventure! We will see tomorrow ; as soon as we arrive in Essaouira, we buy 2 return tickets straight away, ok ?
- OK ! my friend tells me.

This is his first trip.

Departure for Essaouira at 5 am, we settle in the bus; on the road there were lots of holes, so there was a risk of accidents.

We admire the landscapes for 2 hours.

On arrival in Essaouira, the wind was blowing hard and the air was fresh; wow ! There was a big difference in temperature between Marrakech and Essaouira. Quickly we bought two tickets for the return trip, phew we had them! We strolled in the port and the fort then in the small town; a small path with beautiful houses attracted us, we continued and then we got lost; there were no street names or signs; ouch! We looked quickly so as not to miss the return; luckily the sun saved us: I remembered that it was behind me in the morning, so we did the opposite; it worked phew !!

At the hotel there was a swimming pool; Céline and I took advantage of it from time to time. One day I was sitting by the water with my friend soaking our feet; it was cool, we were chatting, suddenly a Moroccan called me patting my leg, he saw us chatting in sign language and he guessed that we were deaf, he told me while miming :
- Hello.
- Hello.
- Beautiful silhouette! Beautiful woman ! he told me.
- Thank you !

I turned to Celine to continue our conversation at the same time as I was running away from this guy who was hitting on me; he didn't interest me. He tapped me on the leg again, mimicking me:
- Can we go for a walk together tonight?
- No thanks !
- Can we dance together tonight ?
- No thank you, I'm deaf.
- No problem, I'm teaching you to dance.
- Oh no ! I do not dance ! I said.
- Can we go for a walk tonight? he repeated.
-
- No thank you, I can't see anything at night! I got on my nerves because he still insisted and didn't leave us alone.
- I accompany you without letting go.
- No, I do not want !

- Would you marry me ?
- No, I have a husband in France! I lied.
- No problem, leave it! Come on, please.
- No.

    I turned to Celine but she had disappeared; shit ! She must have been furious and she was gone to her room. So I walked out of the pool ignoring the guy and, outside our bedroom door, I knocked; my friend opened and I told her :
- Why did you run away without me? Thank you for your help !
- This guy is boring, he lacks respect!
- You remember that a deaf Moroccan warned us that Moroccans flirt with white women; they must therefore be ignored.
- Easy to say ; he talked to you a lot.
- I remained patient, but I always refused his proposals; I'm not crazy, you know it very well and oh! You are jealous hee hee !
- Pff !!
- Come on, ok ?
- I can't take it anymore !
- What is happening ?
- Since our arrival in Morocco, I constantly hear the horns, the guys who flirt with me, "welcome to Morocco, you are beautiful etc ..." It's too much! It's tiring !
- Really, all day ?

- Yes !! Celine told me.
- Ah OK ! I had nothing to do with it and I know that I am lucky to be deaf; but, look, me, a guy was hitting on me earlier; I understand you, let's be strong and ignore them! OK !!
- OK ! Sorry for getting upset and leaving without informing you.
- OK ! It is not serious ! I said.

We hugged each other for comfort and calmed down.

We booked a jeep with the hotel receptionist to go to Ouarzazate.

In a jeep in the middle of the desert, the landscapes were unforgettable and splendid, the dromedaries wandered in the middle of the desert, we imagined ourselves as in the film Lawrence of Arabia, the sun was shining, not a cloud, it was calmer than in the others cities, ideal for Celine.

On returning to France, Céline wrote to me :
- Well, it's calmer, not a word.
- Hee hee! Your ears are not dead yet hi !
- Yes! It makes me feel good !!
- Did you have a good trip anyway ?
- Yes it was beautiful and it's a good memory.
- Phew! Me too !
- I was happy to be with you.
- Me too, I smile.

Chapter 9

Egypt - 2006

I organized my trip to Egypt through the "Travel Cheaper" site; with my deaf friend Christelle, we communicated only in sign language; this is the first time she has been to Africa. We wanted to take an eight day cruise at the end of April on the Nile with excursions included, except an optional visit from Luxor to Aswan in southern Egypt.

At the airport near Bordeaux, I searched my backpack to find a piece of paper to give to the « Marmara » counter and then I asked Christelle :
- Give me your passport, please !
- To do what ?
- To prove that it is us and also that our passports are valid in order to collect papers like our plane tickets.
- Oh ok ; Here's my passport !
- Thank you.
  At the counter, a lady asked us :
- Please, your paper and your passports !
- Here they are !

The lady looked for a bundle of papers, checked our passports and returned a bundle with our passports to me, saying :
- Here are the papers: plane tickets, hotel and cruise papers, and your passports; you have to go to check-in, and have a safe trip !
- Thank you.

When we checked in, we put our suitcases on the conveyor belt, I showed our plane tickets; our suitcases weighed less than twenty-two kilograms, and everything was recorded. Christelle asked me :
- Please, can you put my passport with yours in your money self ?
- OK no problem.

To get the visa, at the airport in Egypt, we gave a paper to fill in with lots of details about our passports, the customs put the stamp with the visa, everything was in order, no need to go through the embassy in Paris. It depends on the country for visas.

For the Nile cruise, to go to Luxor which is in the center of Egypt, we were put in a cabin at the bottom of the boat; I could feel the engine noise from the vibrations; all of a sudden, Christelle began to search everywhere with suspicion; I was surprised to see her like that, I did not understand and questioned her :
- Did you lose something ?

- No.
- What are you looking for ?
- I'm not searching ; uh! Please check under these beds.
- See what ?
- Uh ... if there isn't a snake.
- Bah! We're on a boat, so there is no snake.
- Please look !
- Ok I'm doing it for you.

    I took my flashlight, looked everywhere under the beds, felt the duvets and then in the bathroom, especially in the toilet bowl.
- There is nothing, it's good ok ! I told her.
- OK ! OK !
- Are you afraid of snakes, is that a phobia ?
- Yes, it's horror.
- Why didn't you tell me !
- Uh! I didn't want to say it.
- Well ! We're going for a walk around the wharf.
- Ok not far !
- Yes of course ! Do not worry.
- Please stay close to me !
- Yes, no problem ! I sighed at her.

    On the banks of the Nile, there were small shops; objects, statues, pyramids, sphinxes attracted us, I wanted to buy some souvenirs, Christelle asked the merchant for prices by miming and writing the figures :
- Price ?
- Twenty euros.

She informed me and I replied :
- No, it's better in pounds in Egyptian currency.
- Why ?
- We changed our money for that, and also we have to haggle.
- What to haggle?
- You have to negotiate to agree on the price.
- It is not possible.
- Yes ! We can.
- Is that so ! Go yourself.
- OK no worries.

I negotiated with the merchant using numbers.
- How much does it cost ?
- Twenty euros.
- No in pounds !
- One hundred pounds.

I looked at the paper on which I had written the values for 1, 2.3 ... euros, I showed it to Christelle: one hundred pounds was worth 2 euros and I accepted this price. A couple of tourists took the same thing as me, the merchant asked them for fifty euros; Christelle was shocked, she told me:
- This merchant is a thief !
- No, he trades according to the clothes of the tourists; he is free, that's why we have to negotiate the prices and especially to lower and not give in.
- Pff !
- It's like that. Well, let's continue, ok ?
- OK.

We continued to shop even though there were no windows. For a moment, Christelle pointed to something that had attracted her; I saw his finger and thought to myself: No !! Too late ! Merchants rushed around us; Christelle started to get angry, I whispered to her in signs :
- Stay calm !
- Why are they around us? she got upset.
- Calm down ! You have shown things with your finger; for them it's a sign that you are interested.
- Whore ! We are deaf, it is in our culture to point the finger at.
- Do not forget that we are in Egypt, the finger has an important meaning for them and please take control !
- OK ! she exclaimed, furious.

I mimed them no and asked to push themselves, with a stern face. We are finally out of the harassment of the merchants. In shock, Christelle wanted to get into the boat; it started badly for her! It is normal, it was his first trip to a poor country, and what is more to Africa.

Once in the cabin, Christelle asked me again :
- Check if there is a snake !
- Oh no, it's not true, you're not going to ask me that all day, every day.
She shut up and sulked.

We sailed on the Nile towards Edfu for a distance of fifty kilometers. We stopped to take a tour with the hearing group; it was my first time participating in a hearing group, it was a good experience for me. During the visit to the spectacular site of Karnak, a destroyed temple, the guide explained the story in French, but Christelle and I did not understand anything, we could not follow, so we took the opportunity to take photographs. The group moved away from us but we caught up with them without a problem. At one point the guide got angry with us because we weren't staying in the group and we weren't moving forward with the group; Christelle took out some paper and a pen, and she wrote :
- You know that we are deaf, you ignore us, so we admire this temple and will join you without problem.
- No, you have to stay in a group because the path is complicated, you can get lost easily.
- When you explain to them, what do we do?
- Uh!
- Then you can write to explain us a little about this temple.
- Ok, I'm doing my best but the group is asking for me.
- We must share !
- OK I understand ; Please stay with the group, and I'll put the story down for you in writing.
- OK perfect !

We continued the visit, the guide gave us a summary, it was better than nothing. This temple was huge, the pharaoh had lived there. I motioned to Christelle :
- Look on the walls and even on the columns.
- It's pretty.
- No, look closely, there are writings, pictograms; If you want, there are Egyptian symbols everywhere, not a wall is smooth, without symbols.
- Oh yes it's true, we see a man with the head of an eagle, a horse etc....
- Yes unbelievable, it's like writing a book on the walls.
- It's crazy.
- These symbols are precious about the pharaohs.

The boat sailed on the Nile, and upon arrival in Edfu, I admired the large improvised floating market surrounding the boats waiting to pass the lock. Oh what pollution! It's a shame! It was time to go visit the prestigious Temple of Horus, I had to pass over five boats while walking on small planks; ouch! I risked falling into the Nile because I have difficulty walking straight, especially on the very narrow bridge, because of my balance problems and my reduced visual field; phew! Every time I crossed the boat, men helped me across.

You know crocodiles live in the Nile and even a giant 6-meter crocodile.

During the visit of the temple of Horus, the falcon god, the guide forgot us; we therefore photographed without following the group; we admired more than they did, without getting lost. Paf! At one point there were two entrances; but through which our group had passed? I randomly pulled the left passage, and in a few minutes we were back to our group; how lucky we were! This temple was huge, there were lots of rooms.

I was like, I can't imagine that, it was a big job making these temples, poor slaves !! It must have been very hard to push a large stone with the help of rolling woods, under the lashes; it was horrible back then; it's easier now, with cranes.

Back on the boat, it was our turn to pass the Esna lock created in 1994; wow! It was impressive, we opened the first door, we went through and then we closed that first door; the water was drained to the ideal level to open the second door; it took a whole hour.

During the night, the boat sailed 180 kilometers to Kom Ombo; there, we visited a temple located some five minutes walk: this original and rare temple has two shrines respectively dedicated to Sobek, the Crocodile God.

After visiting this temple, we took a horse-drawn carriage ride; when we stopped, a little boy asked us by miming and showing them to us :
- Please, a twenty euro bill in exchange for one euro coins.
- Why ? Christelle asked me.
- The bank refuses to change euro coins into pounds.
- Ah! That's why !
- Be careful, don't give a ticket too quickly when you exchange.
- Why ?
- I just saw a very angry couple.
- What happened ?
- The boy took the note and ran away without giving the coins.
- Oh, the dishonest !
- First, he puts the coins in my hands, then you give him the bill, and wait until I've hidden the coins.
- OK !

I acted out to the little boy :
- Put your coins in my hands, she will give you a ticket.
- OK ! 1 2 3 4 5 6 7 8 ... 20.
- Its good.

Christelle returned the note and the boy thanked us; the couple told us :
- Ah, you're not stupid! We got screwed, pff! Next time, we'll do as you do, but still he's a thief!
- Yes I saw you! I tell them.
Here they swear by euros.
It's poverty !
Unfortunately, yes ! It's sad.

In Luxor it was the last day, in the morning the guide informed us :
- You must bring the suitcases at ten o'clock at the reception; then we will have lunch at the hotel at noon, then, at one in the afternoon, we will go to the airport but we still do not know the departure time of the plane.

A few people started to grumble and I didn't understand why; So I wrote to a lady :
- What is happening ?
- We are leaving early tomorrow morning at 3 a.m. but we still don't know when the plane will take off.
- Is that so ! It's weird.
- Yes.
- Why are people angry ?
- Some couples have left their children with family or a babysitter or their friends, and they have to pick them up tonight.
- Ouch! It's a mess.
- Yes pff ! ...

- But in the meantime where are we going? Because we have to leave the cruise at 10 o'clock ?
- No it's postponed to 3 p.m. we drop the suitcases here, then we are transferred to the hotel with a free dinner.
- OK, thanks.

At a quarter to three in the afternoon, we left our suitcases at reception; cool ! At three o'clock in the afternoon, a couple panicked and grumbled at the guide, then another couple too; I did not understand, I dared to ask a person in writing :
- What's going on ?
- Their suitcases are missing.
- Is that so ! How come ?
- There are some flight errors.
- Ah darn !!
- Are your suitcases there ?
- Yeah, we put them down a few minutes ago!
- Check anyway !
- OK, thanks.

Christelle and I checked and saw that my suitcase had also disappeared, we made a complaint to the guide.

Oh my, it's poorly organized: so in all five suitcases left by mistake by bus for 250 kilometers. My God ! I'm in shorts and a sleeveless T-shirt, I'm going to be cold tonight here or in France; luckily I have our passports.

At the hotel, after dinner, many stayed outside, worrying about the five suitcases and also about the time of the flight. At 11:30 pm, finally my suitcase returned after an adventure of 500 kilometers in the desert; I was relieved. Hop! In the bedroom, I dressed warmly and then we stayed together outside.

At 3 am, the guide called us to go by bus to the airport; then, once at the airport, I looked at the board, but it was all empty; it was abnormal, we followed the band to the recording; I saw two different airports for the arrival: Orly and CDG Roissy; the guide told us first "to Orly" then "to CDG"; It was a mess, everyone was starting to get excited with the fatigue and disorganization. Christelle and I stayed in the line for Orly because this plane left at 5 am and the other for CDG at 5:45 am. Phew! We had two tickets for Orly and went to customs and then to the waiting room; I looked for the painting, it was still empty; I felt the vibrations of the speakers; pff! They made an announcement at the microphone; since we are deaf, so I asked someone in my group :
- There was an announcement on the microphone, we are deaf, are you going to Orly ?
- Yes, I'm warning you, okay.
- Thank you.
At five in the morning, the microphone woke me up, a person informed us that we were going

there, we took the bus to the plane, I noticed that there was something wrong because the make of the plane was "Corsaire"; I found this weird and warned Christelle :
- I don't feel it, look at the mark.
- Corsair, what's the problem ?
- Look at our tickets.
- It does not say "privateer", it wrote Air Egypt.
- I think there is a mistake.
- No, it's okay.
- Ok, you'll see !
- Stopped ! she scolded me.

   I got on the plane and then the hostess asked for my ticket because I was in front, so I showed her, the hostess forced us to get off and go to the waiting room; my group got more and more upset, they refused to come down and wanted to go back to France. I said to Christelle :
- You see !
- You piss me off !
- Well, I had nothing to do with it, it was the organization that did its job poorly.
- Yes, it's true ! Excuse me.

   It was a hassle! We returned unhappy to the waiting room, we were told our flight would be at 7 am. The tension was mounting, we acted like a strike by preventing the others from leaving. The flight to CDG got off to a good start on time. The guards came to calm us down.

Concern grew because we wondered when we would take off; I paced around to stay awake and the group chatted together to make a complaint to the agency; we signed a petition. At 7 am our flight was announced, one of our group checked with the hostess to make sure we were going home; the answer was yes. Phew! Finally we flew to Paris.

Chapter 10

Australia in 2011 - 2012

December 22, 2011 was a big day for me; finally my dream was coming true: I had wanted to go to Australia for over twenty years. My large backpack was ready. My friend Stéphanie took me from Poitiers train station to Roissy Charles de Gaulle airport in Paris. It was very kind of him, I felt reassured and also safe not to miss the plane, since my eyesight had diminished.

The TGV arrived at the airport in the basement of Terminal 2; it was convenient. I was in front of the recording; a month before leaving, I had booked someone to accompany me when changing planes, especially for the transfer to Dubai, given my double sensory handicap. I showed some papers and my validated passport to a hostess I assumed was from Dubai because of her dark skin tone and everything was recorded; my large backpack that weighed 10 kg went on the treadmill, and Wow! I got the tickets for Dubai and Melbourne! My flight was going to last thirty-two and a half hours with a stopover in Dubai and ten hours of jet lag. My tension and my emotion mounted.

    The hour struck, an attendant came to pick me up to go through customs and then to the waiting room and I said to Stéphanie :
- Ah ! It's time ; bye, see you in five weeks ok
- Have a nice trip ! Make the most of it ! Take lots of great photos and email a few to me ! OK ?
- Without fail !

    We walked away. Customs checked my passport and plane tickets, everything was in order; I was in the waiting room; in the meantime, I have texted Stéphanie :
- Thank you for coming with me. Kisses.
- You're welcome ! This is completely normal, enjoy it! Kisses.

    The guide called me to tell me it was time to get on the plane; I was well seated by the window, unfortunately it was already dark; I put my new iPhone that I bought 3 weeks ago into airplane mode, it was my first time using the touch keyboard.
    During the flight from Paris to Dubai in the United Arab Emirates, once the plane had taken off, the hostess showed me the menu to choose dinner, I chose the chicken, then the lights went out.

I managed to sleep when I usually never sleep when traveling regardless of the means of transport.

On arrival in Dubai, the hostess told me to wait a bit: a guide would come and pick me up to transfer me. A few minutes later, everything was empty on the plane except the hostesses and me, I worried a little bit because it was the first time that a guide took care of me, but I had already done so in France in the TGV.

Finally the guide arrived with a fluorescent vest and a walkie-talkie; he went with me, and as I got off the plane he said :
- Get into the wheelchair !
- Oh no !
- If it is necessary !
- No. I have two legs to walk and I simply take your elbow! I tell him mimicking and with a little English.
- OK !

The guide spoke into the walkie-talkie and walked me through customs and then to the other plane; we walked for a very long time - wow! Dubai Airport was huge, it's the third in the world, it was built in 2000, everything is modern! After 20 minutes on foot, I was in a closed waiting room. But I was with foreign children from several countries seen the faces and the outfits.

In thoughts, I said to myself: yet I am not a child! I am just deaf and visually impaired, I believe there is a mistake. But OK !

In the meantime, I turned on my iPhone and connected to the WIFI, Ah! It worked and it was free, so I called my Australian friend Usher, Alison, by skype; without success. I was confusing the schedules! Fortunately I saw the international hours. Ah darn ! She was still sleeping! I sent Stéphanie a text message to reassure her:
- Welcome to Dubai. All is well and everything went well with the guide. Kisses.

Four hours of waiting have passed. An attendant came to pick me up to transfer me to the flight to Melbourne.
Sixteen more hours of flight! My record was broken with a flight time of thirty-two hours and a half! It's been over a day! It is enormous ! So I had lost a day.
Here I am well installed on the plane, still near the window. The smiling hostess gave me a safety book in English in Braille and large print; I was surprised, I could read it, it was great !

In my thoughts I said to myself: this is great, but why not in France? Oh ! I notice that France is always behind on accessibility !

The plane took off ; an hour later, after a small dinner on Dubai time, the lights suddenly went out, it was pitch dark. Ouch! It was too late to go to the toilet! What to do ? Too bad, I took my iPhone and typed in English :
- Hello madam, I am deafblind, French and you ?
I showed my message to my neighbor, she took her iPhone, answered me and showed me her answer :
- Hello, I am from Iran and you are going to Australia for tourism or work ?
- Tourism with my friend. And you ?
- Me too.
- Can you come with me to the bathroom, please ?
- OK no problem.
She guided me to the bathroom and I begged her, mimicking :
- Wait please !
- Ok, she smiles at me.

I hurried away for fear that it would disappear. Phew! She was still there. Then, in turn, I waited for her, then we returned to our seats together, and continued our conversation with our iPhones. It was nice !

Suddenly the hostess brought drinks, I couldn't see anything because everything was dark; the Iranian woman informed me by mimicking that there was fruit juice. I dabbled, I almost knocked over the tray with lots of glasses in it; luckily the iranian grabbed my hand, then put a drink in my hand. I thanked them. Phew !! It could have been a disaster! Then I fell asleep again ...

I was like: it's good that I can continue to travel because of the accessibility and also because I can write in English; but, during the flight, it is not easy to communicate with the hostess; it would be nice if the hostesses knew how to sign, but it's better than nothing ...

The light came back on, it was breakfast time and we were arriving in Melbourne. Oh there ! The hour was drawing near! I was all excited, I couldn't wait to get there because I was starting to get fed up with being in the seat all this time.

The plane landed on December 24 at 6:20 am: here I am in Australia. I couldn't realize that my dream had been achieved; the hostess warned me to wait, that an attendant was coming. I turned on my iPhone. Ouch! My battery was almost dead! An attendant arrives with a walkie-talkie who announces to me in English :

- Welcome to Australia.
- Thank you. I smiled.

She accompanies me through customs and then collects my backpack. We were in front of the conveyor belt for the suitcases, I had easily spotted my bright yellow backpack, it was the only one, it was lucky. We were heading towards the exit when suddenly the guide braked before the exit door; I wondered what was going on, the guide told me :
- Put your bags on the ground !
- Ah OK ! I said.

I turned to see around me. Ah! There was a line of 10 people, the luggage on the ground; I saw a dog like in the movie "Colombo", he smelled all the luggage; I understood, it was to stop people who carry drugs; it was my turn, I had confidence in myself because I don't do drugs; everything was settled, I took my bags back.

I thought to myself: wow! Customs are stricter than in other countries, I wonder if there is a lot of drug trafficking here? I'll ask Alison to find out more.

Here I am at the exit, right in front of my friend Alison and her husband Ross; we hugged each other with joy. We went to collect the car from the parking lot; on the sidewalk, I lay down on the ground to say that I was good in Australia, imitating the Pope !!!

In the parking lot, I put my backpack in the trunk, I got in behind, then remembered that the steering wheel was reversed, ie on the right like in England. This is normal, Australia is still an English colony as the flag has a small flag of England. The weather was nice, it was summer; it was funny because in the evening it would be Christmas, in the middle of summer! So Santa Claus would wear red shorts like in the "Malibu Alert" series !

I asked Alison :
- Do you mind that I'm walking around with my white cane ?
- Not at all ! How long have you been using it ?
- In March, I did a locomotion course, it helps me a lot, I look less and less at the ground because the tip of the cane warns me that there are obstacles or holes ... and also I no longer hit people; it calms me down because, before, I would hit people every time without doing it on purpose because my visual field is weak; they always yelled at me, it annoyed me, like I was a thug! Pff! Then in April, I did an internship with the electronic cane.

- Are you comfortable in front of people with your white cane ?
- At first, people's stares got on my nerves, like I was weird, and now I don't care: it's important to protect myself !
- It's just ! Uh! What is the difference between the white cane and the electronic cane ?
- Good question !! The white cane is the simple cane that all the blind have and the electronic cane warns me by vibration when I approach a stopped car or a pole or people etc. ..., at a distance of 'about one to three meters.
- Ah ! Is the electronic white cane effective ?
- Yes and no, but there are flaws.
- What flaws ?
- For example, on a fairly wide sidewalk, my electronic cane warns me that there is something approaching, I look around me especially in front of course, I do not see where the obstacle is, I tell myself how weird, I continue, it still vibrates; I found the problem, the sun was shining, hitting a license plate and then reflecting off the housing of my electronic cane.
- Ah darn !
- And also it's not easy, when I walk around, the tip of my white cane rubs on the ground and tells me about the type of ground: concrete or lawn or etc. ... and with the electronic cane, it vibrates too much, it's not easy to know what's in front, you know ?

- Yes I see !
- I prefer the simple white cane, that's it !!
- I get it !
- A question: at customs, control is very strict, is it because of drug trafficking ?
- Yes, that's right, that's right, coming from Bali, Indonesia, Thailand ...
- Oh ok !

We took the road to visit Alison's sister who had come to my house in September 2011 with Alison, we went to Fish Creek, east of Victoria, one of the 6 states of Australia; I saw on the flag that there are 6 stars, we were going to celebrate Christmas together.

Why in French and Australian sign language do we make the sign "Australia" by taking something on the left with the thumbs and middle fingers that we carry to the right and then let go? Here's a little story: the English had sailed and found a large unknown island; so they took it as a colony and named it « Australia ». To build roads and towns they transported English prisoners and handicapped people to Australia; it is as if the English wanted to get rid of the wrong people. Then the Australians were unhappy with the English and they wanted to become independent, but without success.

On her sister's huge farm, we find cows different from those in France, horses ..., Alison told me :
- Looked ! Kangaroos !
- Wow! In the middle of nature ?
- Yes, they are free.

I rushed to take pictures, amazing !! As in France, deer, wild boar .... They were free.
We wandered around; despite my great fatigue from the 10 hours of jet lag, I needed to let off steam after 32h30 of flight.

In the evening, after dinner, no Christmas Eve, it's not like in France: the Christmas party begins on December 25 and lasts until December 26 in the evening. I got into bed at 8:30 am, completely knocked out.

On Christmas day, up at 8:30 am, I felt great, the sun was shining and it was hot; lunchtime was barbecue, it's cool for Christmas day and fun. In the afternoon Alison, her nephew and I went shellfish fishing in a jeep to a small freshwater lake, in their farm of "yabbies", crustaceans with a body that looks like a mixture of prawns and langoustines and with claws like crabs but small. His nephew explained to me how to separate females and males by observing their bodies; only the males are taken because the females continue to reproduce.

After Christmas Alison, Ross and I visited Sanremo by the sea, we were in the harbor, I admired the pelicans and the transparent sea; I saw a giant triangle shaped thing with a long tail, it was a giant stingray. Alison explained to me in sign language :
- This giant ray is dangerous, its tail is used to defend itself as one throws arrows in archery; and the tip of its tail contains poison like a snake.
- How many centimeters is that a sting ?
- Twenty centimeters; if she has used it before, it grows back from two centimeters to a maximum of twenty centimeters.
- If someone calmly approaches to touch, is it possible ?
- Yes, it is possible but be careful not just any old way !
- Ah ! Explain to me please.
- Ok. To touch it, you have to stand in front of the giant stingray so that it can see you and be reassured; if you get behind, she is afraid and defends herself, like other animals.
- Ah! OK, I get it.
- I have 2 stories to tell you.
- I can't wait to learn more.

- First famous story in Australia: a famous man named Steve Irwin, zoologist and television host, had created a zoo like no other near Brisbane; he protected the animals by giving them a little freedom. He wanted to make a film about giant rays; he goes to sea with a cameraman, they get ready to dive; Steve sees a giant stingray, he comes closer on his back, the cameraman tells him in mime not to get too close, Steve does not listen to him, lies on the back of the giant stingray and, suddenly, receives the sting in full chest launched by the giant ray; he is shocked, loses control, the cameraman swims to save Steven but, on the boat, Steven panics, he removes the sting.
- Ah ! He should not be removed, he had to be taken to the hospital; ouch! Then ?
- Well, he died on September 4, 2006. When the Australians found out, some got mad at the giant stingrays, a few killed them.
- Oh my God ! But Steve made a mistake by landing on the back of the giant stingray. And the second story ?
- My 72-year-old uncle is a fisherman, in his family they have been for generations; one day, on the boat, he hauls back fish with a huge net; he is used to giant rays, he takes them by the tail; suddenly, a giant stingray throws its sting which touches his leg, his son makes him lie down and reassures him to stay calm, because

my uncle was panicking. At the hospital, the sting was removed, he was saved but, for 3 days, his injured leg remained paralyzed asleep, then he resumed walking little by little, and now he is walking normally.
- Phew !! I said.
- I have some other interesting information to tell you about turtles, which can be found in North East Australia.
- Ah turtles! Small or giant ?
- Yes it is important to protect turtles because they eat jellyfish; but the big problem is that people throw plastic in the sea, and turtles eat them because they think they're jellyfish, they're wrong; they therefore fall ill and then die of suffocation.
- Oh my god ! We must stop throwing plastics in the sea.
- Good news: professionals are working to protect animals; they know when the turtles are nesting, they hide near the beach before sunset to watch the places where the turtles lay their eggs.
- Why in the evening ?
- Turtles lay their eggs at night in the sand.
- Oh ok !
- When the turtles leave for the sea, the professionals collect the eggs delicately because the eggs are fragile, they wrap them well to avoid breaking them.

- Oh no ! They must be left in the wild.
- The eggs must be protected; Why ? Let me explain: if we leave the eggs in the middle of nature, when the babies come out of the eggs, they walk on the sand to go to the sea, the birds can then eat them; then, in the sea, the sharks too.
- Ah! I understand better.
- Professionals take eggs, about 50 to 100 eggs, almost half, to the farm; they put them in the sand, cover them well to keep them warm, then the babies take out eggs and go into a small lake of seawater as if it were near the beach. Once they've grown, at the right time, the pros take them back to the real beach and let them go. So birds and sharks cannot eat them; on the other hand, turtles eat jellyfish. If the professionals did not do this, the turtles would be endangered and also the jellyfish would grow more and more.

I told myself that it is important to protect animals and also nature; I had just learned about turtles and jellyfish etc ...; in the world there is a lack of information on these subjects, it's a shame !!

Please protect animals and nature.

It was lunchtime, we were at the restaurant, Alison had translated the menu for me; So, to the cashier, I pointed to the menu I had chosen, the cashier said :
- Twenty AUD (Australian dollar)
   I paid, then the cashier gave me a little iron sign with the number, I wondered what it was for, Alison informed me :
- Go and settle where you want, I'll explain.
- OK no problem.

   I settled in with my number, Alison and Ross joined me. While waiting for our set, Alison explained to me :
- In Australia, when we go to a restaurant, bar or cafe, we first choose the menu or a dish or something else then we pay, we give you a number, and the waiter brings the plate to your table thanks to the number.
- Poor waiter! He has to look for the numbers to give the plates, it's a waste of time.
- Uh !
- Yeah, look, there are two rooms, one inside and one outside.
- Oh that's right !

   The waiter brought me my meal, I noticed there was a mistake and called him back. Yes ! He was wrong; oh hell! Phew! My plate was served.

- You see it's not practical, given the errors I whispered.
- It's rare and this is the first time I've seen it.
- Ah I am the devil hee hee! Or I bring bad luck.
- LOL.

We left for the « Australia Wild Life » park, a kind of zoo; I saw kangaroos in the wild, I approached to try to stroke them, with the fear of receiving a punch; Alison reassured me :
- Don't be afraid, he won't punch his paws.
- But I've seen movies where kangaroos are boxing !
- It's wrong ; if someone annoys or assaults him, yes, he kicks or he scratches with his upper paws.
- Ah ok that's clear ! Please film me with my iphone thank you !

I approached confidently, I held seeds in my hand, the kangaroo ate in my hand, and at the same time I stroked it. Wow! It was too cute and cute, his hair was soft, and I didn't scare him. I have noticed that there are different species of kangaroos depending on color, size and shape.
- Are there different races ?
- Yes that's right, there are 65 breeds in Australia! There we see a "gray kangaroo", there a « red kangaroo » ...
- Wow that's huge !!
- Look at the little one in the pocket, it's so cute.
- Is that an emu over there ?

- Yes.

The emu is close to the ostrich, but without the wings; I held out my hand to him with seeds in it, I tried to stroke him, it was not easy, he was very agitated, like he was afraid.
- Look at the koalas! Alison told me.
- Or ?
- In the tree above !
- I did not find.
- Wait, Ross is going to show you with his camera.
- OK !

I spotted first on the camera and then in real life; Oh ! It wasn't easy because of the lack of contrast.

It is not easy to spot the animals due to the lack of contrast; luckily new technologies are helping me a lot, for example the camera or the iphone, by doing zooms.

We continued on to The Nobbies to admire the penguins by the sea; there was a strong icy wind coming from the south; we must not forget that we are in the southern hemisphere, so it's the opposite, and also close to Antarctica (south pole). On the road, lots of red-skinned kangaroos, called "wallaby", were roaming free; we risked crushing them or, by hitting them, shattering the windows or damaging the bodywork; so we drove slowly.

At the "Wilson Promontry National Park" campsite, we were by the sea, near a river with also trails for hiking; in 1945, during world war ii against japan, there was a camp and an airport there and no houses or shops had yet been built, there were only tents and caravans to preserve nature . At lunch, Alison, Ross and I walked into a store where there was a fast food restaurant, I read the menu: there were only names of fish in English that I did not know; So Alison advised me :
- Taste the fish flake with fries, it's delicious !
- Ouch! I've never eaten a shark ! I said.
- Huh! At your place, I tasted snails, gizzards, cheeses etc. ... So it's your turn!
- Uh! It is true ! Ok I take this !

On a wooden table, I tasted a small piece of shark and then loved it, it was really delicious and light. At the beach, the sand was very white and soft, like cornmeal. Alison informed me that in Australia there are plenty of varieties of sands.

For 45 minutes we crossed a large bay from the south on a boat that carried cars and tourists to go to the other side, from Sorrento to Queen Cliff, the Fort Queen Cliff military area; Melbourne lies to the north of this large bay. I asked Alison questions in sign language :

- It's huge, I see the exit to the sea from the south; are we free to go out or in ?
- Yes and no !
- Why yes and no ?
- We are not completely free because at the border there are mines, in shallow water, which date from the Second World War with Japan.
- Why not defuse these mines ?
- We prefer to leave them to protect us.
- So we can't go out or in ?
- Yes, we can, but when we want to go in or out, we have to phone the Coast Guard and then wait for a Coast Guard boat to accompany us; but you have to follow it, especially keep the same direction because the coastguard boat has a camera to avoid hitting the mines.
- Ah OK ! But foreigners don't know there are mines, it goes unnoticed! Ouch !!
- At the corner of the beach, there are soldiers, like coast guards, who watch and arrest people as at customs and take information.
- Can sharks come in ?
- Yes !
- So we can't swim freely.
- Yes ! But there are a few safe beaches, I'll show you soon.
- OK ! No problem !
- When you are on a sailboat, you have to follow the right direction because there is a very

strong and dangerous current, like a vacuum cleaner. Like everywhere, in lakes etc.

Several beaches in this large bay have been secured against sharks: we have created low dams with iron fences at the top to be able to see the sea or the sails etc, so that we can swim but this is not not big.

In the evening, in Geelong, at Alison's, I finally connected to the WIFI, I sent an email to Stéphanie to reassure her, tell her that everything was going well, with some photos and especially the video where I was stroking a kangaroo ; I also sent some to my parents who were worried about it after 5 days of silence on my part.

My iPhone's battery was dead, I plugged it in with the French-Australian plug that Alison had bought; I saw that unfortunately it was not charging, so I changed the take, in another room, it was still the same, so I asked Alison :
- Excuse me ! I think the plugs are not working.
- Is that so ! Wait, I'm checking with your iPhone.
- OK ....
- It works !
- I do not understand ! Just now I plugged it in there.
- Ah! You have to press a small switch near the sockets.

- Okay, but why are there light switches ?
- For security purposes ; here we have 240 volts.
- Oh okay, and in France 220 V; It's really a good idea ; It's awesome.
- Yes, it's convenient.
  But at your sister's, I plugged it in without any problem.
- Ah! Maybe she forgot to turn off the plugs.

   In Geelong, Alison and I were resting, so we took a walk by the river; I was startled when I saw the sign warning of the danger of snakes.
- Ah! Are there snakes everywhere ?
- Yes it depends on the days and where.
- Are they dangerous ?
- Yes and no.
- Ah OK ! What about crocodiles ?
- No, not in South Australia !
- Oh ok but where ?
- In the East and more in the North.
- Tarantulas?
- No, not here, we find them in the North-East and dangerous spiders everywhere.
- Can we die ?
- It depends ; when they sting, people have swollen, hollow-shaped pimples, itchy and then they get sick, with a fever. So it is better to close drawers, cupboards, laundry baskets and bins.

- Ouch, Ushers can't see well, it's not easy.
- Fair enough, that's the problem; that's why we have to close everything.
- Okay and why are the windows and doors lined with mosquito nets ?
- It is against mosquitoes, flies, wasps, spiders; no need for insect repellants, except for wasps which can enter quickly when you open the doors to get inside; and in Ayers Rock it's worse, there are a lot of flies, you'll see.
- OK !

    I said to myself: I understand better, I have seen on sites that in Australia many people are killed by dangerous animals; I found it weird because I thought it was in Africa, but no, it is in Australia ...

    On December 31, 2011, Alison and I went to Melbourne to tour the city then see her friends and then the fireworks. It was 38 degrees in the shade; in the morning we visited the tower which is called the Eureka Tower; it has 92 floors; we took the elevator to the 88th floor in 38 seconds to admire the whole city: I saw the Formula 1 track, stadiums: Australian football, cricket, tennis, trains ... then we walked around in town, Alison offered to go see some stadiums.
- Yes it's far ?
- No, it's 150 meters away.

- Oh super ok !
- Here are the tennis stadiums: Australian Open.
- Where is the new stadium ?
- This stadium dates from 2001.
- Wow that's great! What year did the old tennis stadiums open ?
- In 1988 and there, the cricket stadium !
- Ah it's close, it's convenient.
- Yes and in 1956 the Olympic cricket games were held here.
- Awesome !
- There, the Australian football stadium.

It's so great, everything is close and convenient for travel and also for accessibility !

In the afternoon, we joined his friends at the bar where I made acquaintances, suddenly I saw through the window police officers arresting drunks because of their bizarre behavior and Alison explained to me :
- It is legal, before the time of holidays or events, the police arrest drunks to avoid arguments, fights etc ... during the holidays.
- Wow! The law is very strict, but still it protects you and it reassures.

It was time for the fireworks display, it was 30 degrees at 7:30 p.m., public transport stopped working, there were already people, friends and I looked for a place near the river to better see the fireworks. Phew! We got settled in, cool, and the crowd was piling up more and more, it was crazy !! It was funny for me, considering the heat, to see a fireworks display in December; and at 10 p.m. the show started, it was wonderful, I filmed with my iphone. In the end, Alison and I had to take the train back to Geelong; we hurried, unfortunately with all this crowd, we had difficulty crossing especially without getting lost; we didn't let go, it was madness, I wondered how many people there were. Phew !

We managed to take the tram first; ouch! We were tight, I almost fell out because I felt suffocated from the crowd and the heat, I controlled myself and held on; Alison saw that I was not well; upon arrival at the station we exited with relief, I caught my breath calmly and we got on the train at 11:10 pm, and at midnight Alison and I wished each other a Happy New Year 2012 on the train. What a funny tradition! Hi! And that made me funny because I was already passing in 2012, compared to the French who would wait another ten hours to pass in turn in 2012. I still sent SMS by whatsapps to my family and my French friends for their wish 2012 a happy new year and good health. Ross told us that in Melbourne there were 1.5 million people at the fireworks display.

I said to myself: oh there! It's huge 1.5 million people, I admit that I will not do it again because it had not been easy for me: at night, the crowd, it made me anxious, for fear of losing Alison or make us attack or etc... but it is a very good memory !!

On the morning of January 1, 2012, my iphone rang, I had several text messages in whatsapps and emails: that's it, France had passed in 2012. It was sunny and warm; so we went to "Torquay" beach; it was my first swim in Australia, the wind was blowing from the south; first I asked Alison :
- Are there sharks ?
- It is possible but today the air and the sea are fresh so it's okay.
- Ah OK ! I can bathe quietly.
  We bathed, it curdled a bit like at home in "La Manche" in the north or in Brittany.
  Alison told me a true story :
- Before, in Australia, there were no rabbits; one day in 1859, an English family took a boat from England to Australia; on arrival in Australia there is a controller and a wicket, the English woman has taken two boxes full of rabbits, she does not want to pay the taxes; she wears a hoop as under the dresses of yesteryear; she therefore hangs the rabbits around the hoop to hide them, the inspector looks on without searching her and lets her pass. Then this woman

gets into the cart without removing the rabbits out of prudence; after 25 km, the English family moved into a house and then this woman put the rabbits in a cage near the river. One day when it was raining hard, the water level of the river rose, the rabbits therefore fled by swimming thanks to the rising water then they reproduced and since then there are plenty of rabbits in Australia.

In a store, we did some shopping, and I was amazed to see just one small column of cheeses: Feta, Boursin and 2 Australian cheeses.
- Only this ?
- Yes.
- Ah! This is not much compared to France: we have 246 kinds of cheese.
- Look at the price of Roquefort.
- Eighty grams for eleven AUD, how much is that in euros ?
- Seven euros.
- Oh damn ! It's madness, in France we have 150 grams for 2.20 euros.
- It is cheap.
- It's because of the taxes for air travel.
- Yes pff! Alison sighs.

We took the road to Ballarat, 86 kilometers from Geelong, a town with many buildings made of stone like in England and an "Arch memorial of

the war of Victory" monument commemorating the world war in Australia; Alison told me a story:
- This monument explains that there were gold diggers, the British government ordered them to enlist in the army to go to war in Turkey, the names of the dead are displayed on this monument.
- Ok, there are lots of names !
- There is also the main gold bank, Ballarat; it is connected to other towns within an hour's drive.
- Wow! It's a huge bank in Victoria.
- Yes, very fair.
- Where can we find gold ?
- Soveriger Hill is an open-air gold museum, it houses tents, wagons ... You can imagine how it used to be, in 1851, when the gold diggers lived there.
- It's like in Charlot's film « The Gold Rush ».

During the visit, we passed a date, I had an idea all of a sudden: while miming, I begged her to stop and I asked Alison to film me, then I started next to the horse and imitated a cowboy: bang bang! The date looked at me oddly and smiled. I thanked her, checked out the movie and, a little disappointed, said to Alison :
- You move too much !
- Yeah, I laughed while filming you because you were funny and the lady took you for a crazy hee hee !

We burst out laughing like crazy.

Another time, to go to the capital of Australia, Canberra, Alison and I took the train from Melbourne to Albury, 325 km, just on the border between two states: Victoria and New South Wales (NSW), then the bus to Canberra; in all, 662 km. In the train, we were seated side by side with two other people opposite, it was 40 degrees, for a moment the train slowed down, we were worried because we had to take the bus to go to Canberra. A couple in front of us showed me their cellphones, ouch! Unable to read her undersized written message, so I handed Alison her cell phone and saw that the couple weren't happy; So I said to them while miming and speaking at the same time a little in English :
- Excuse me, I'm French.
- Ah! You come from France, welcome to Australia.
- Thank you and my friend is Australian.
- How do you communicate with each other ?
- We exchange in French sign language and Australian sign language.
- Wow Super !!
  - Thank you, I smile.

Alison translated the message into tactile sign language for me because she was too close to

me for me to see her signs; the message said the train was very late, but the bus to Canberra was waiting for us. Phew! I asked Alison :
- Why is the train late ?
- No idea ! The message did not say so.
- Better write to him to find out a little more, please.
- OK ! I'm preparing a message! she said to me.

We spoke with the couple by text message; finally the train was late because of the appalling heat: the rails were melting, we had to travel between 40 and 50 km / h. At the end of our discussion, we thanked them with a smile.

Inside, I thought: these people are very nice to give us information, especially by SMS; it's incredible ! It's very human! In France, it's the opposite, it's a shame !

When the train stopped, Alison and I got off and ran to the bus so as not to miss it; phew! We got on and didn't see anyone on the bus; it was weird, we were the first to sit in front of a giant window so we could admire the scenery; cool ! Then we understood: the bus was waiting for all the travelers, but, all the same, we had done well to run to arrive first, hi! The journey continued on the highway; there were a lot of dead kangaroos.

In Canberra, Alison and I took an organized tour bus, with a route and timetables; it was easier to get around without getting lost.

The first visit was Australia's largest war dead memorial.

The second visit was to the President's house: Alison and I had to go through security and empty our pockets on the conveyor belt; after having passed the security gate, we resumed our business, we had started the visit when, suddenly, a security guard caught Alison who jumped; he showed her a black basket: Alison had forgotten her cell phone in it. I scolded him :
- Be careful ! Luckily, is this agent serious?
- Yes, phew! The problem is, the basket is black and so is my laptop; it's a lack of contrast.
- Yes it's true, it's not practical and the best thing when you go through the security gate is to put your cell phone in your banana! I do that.
- Yes, you're right !
- Great ! This agent is nice and serious! Well, we're going to visit ok ?

The third and last visit was the science museum, it was interesting, it tells the story of the life of the aborigines. Unfortunately at the end of the visit, we couldn't find the exit; we walked around the museum three times without success, we couldn't find a sign indicating the exit, we were panicking because the last bus was coming

soon, Alison missed 3 steps that she had not seen, I caught up with her , phew! She was not hurt.
- Thank you ! Alison told me.
- Haven't you seen the 3 steps ?
- No, it is difficult to see and besides, in the panic, I did not pay attention.
- Please, we stay calm.
- OK !
- Whore ! There are only a few minutes left !!!
- Shit.
- You better ask that lady.
- OK.

The lady showed us the way, we ran and finally we got out well phew !! Just the last bus arrived, we were safe and sound.

Well, we had an early dinner because around the hotel there were no restaurants or shops. Then we looked for the bus to go to the hotel; my god it was a mess and it wasn't clear! Luckily 2 Japanese handed us their ipads to communicate with us; they wanted to help us find the bus number; I was surprised, Alison too; they had seen us angry and also that we were deaf; then Alison said the name of the street of the hotel, one of the Japanese looked up and asked the drivers for the number of the bus; That's it, We had the number and were reassured; we thanked them with a smile and a thumbs up for saying « great ».

Go to Sydney, by bus, 285 km; on arrival we left our bags at the hotel then we went to the meeting point at The Rock which is the oldest district of Sydney to meet a friend of Alison named Eddy who is Usher like us. Eddy came from Perth with his wife and third daughter.

At the edge of the bay, the Sydney Harbor Bridge and the Opera House are very close, it was beautiful and impressive; finally my dream came true to see especially the Opera House; it moved me! We spotted an aboriginal playing an instrument, a « Didgeridoo ».

On the bridge there are eight lanes for cars, two for the railroad, one for cyclists and one for pedestrians, just like on the bridge in New York seen in movies. It was time to climb the bridge, we had an appointment, we were given wetsuits, climbing harnesses and ropes to hang from a wire rope; we had to empty our pockets; our belongings were safely stored. Eddy's hearing daughter served as a communication aid for us as a "coda", meaning daughter of deaf parents.
- Why empty your pockets and ban cameras and laptops? I whispere.

- Because if you are clumsy and you drop an object, there is a big risk of having accidents for the cars which are below.
- Ah OK ! I understand better.

It was a great moment to climb to the top of the bridge with the guide, we were too excited, we, the 3 Ushers, we informed each other: be careful of the bars that we had to step over or under which we had to bow our heads, to steps etc ... To avoid hurting us given our weak visual fields.
- How many stairs are there? I asked.
- 1000 steps! replied the guide.
- Ah! Like the Eiffel Tower in Paris! I said.
The guide explained to us :
- This bridge was built in 1932.
- How long did the work last ?
- Seven years.
- Ah, that's a long time !
- Yes, during the works, there was a level error: the two parts of the bridge did not end up opposite each other; we therefore had to dismantle it and then reassemble it; so we lost a lot of years.
- Ouch it's not easy, and how many meters is this bridge?
- In length: 503 m, in width: 49 m and in height: 134 m.
- Why did we make this bridge ?
- To reduce the number of boats.

Here we are at the top of the bridge, the view was splendid. For the return trip, on the next lane, we had to be very careful because we could not see the steps going down for lack of contrast. Once at the foot of the bridge, everything had gone wonderfully, without injuries, we were all delighted and also we were lucky to have had good weather in the afternoon because it was very cloudy in the morning.

At the Opera House, Alison and I were all alone because Eddy's little family had gone to stay with friends, I approached very close to the Opera House, I was amazed and exclaimed to Alison :
- I thought it was white paint, well no, it's a tile made of small white tiles.
- Hee hee! Yes you had seen badly.
- Unbelievable ! It's a great job and it amazes me !! When was it built ?
- In 1973.
- Ah I was 2 years old! Lol.
- Mimi hee hee !
- We go to the hotel for the shower and then to the restaurant.
- Yes good idea ! I need a little rest and soon it will be dark.
  - Yes, in addition.

We walked through town, Alison led me, I was holding her elbow, what a crowd! Alison hit her-

self several times, it was madness! At the hotel, I chatted with Alison :
- Tomorrow, I will use my white cane and you will hold my elbow please !
- Uh ! OK.
- I saw you angry because of people pushing you.
- People don't pay attention.
- Wait, people don't know we're Usher, do you agree with me ?
- It is true.
- Please calm down; tomorrow I take my white cane, accept !
- Ok I accept.

    The Sydney Tower is the second tallest in Australia, measuring 305 meters, 7 storeys and has been open to the public since 1981. Alison and I climbed the elevator to view Sydney from the 6th floor; we got out of the elevator, disaster everything was black, the tiles, walls, chairs, tables; luckily I had my white cane, but several times people who were not careful bumped into my cane.
- It's nonsense because at the bottom it says "accessibility for the disabled ».
- Yes it's shame and before it was not like that, I'm surprised.

- On the 6th floor, these are shops, hi ! And you can't admire anything, because of the restaurant.
- No, we're going to go even higher, I'm looking for another elevator to go to the 7th floor.
- Like earlier, is it the same ?
- No, another.
- Oh ok ! We will try to locate the sign.
- We couldn't find her, it's weird !
- We will ask the traders; OK ?
- OK.

A shopkeeper gave us an indication, we still have not found the other elevator but a staircase, we tried but it did not go to the right place; we searched again, still without success and asked another trader who accompanied us; finally we have found.
- Oh damn ! This sign is well hidden, pff !
- Pff !
- Yes it's good ; in addition, we go to 7th heaven, hi! I said.
- Mdr.

On the 7th floor, I could admire better. Phew! What a beautiful city !

To get back to the hotel, there was still an incredible crowd, so I pulled out my white cane, we walked straight;   Alison was amazed, people were pushing each other or shouting for attention, they let us pass as if we were queens, we were very quiet, without bumping into each other or making our eyes work, cool !

At the hotel, Alison confessed to me:
- Wow! Too great this white cane !
- It serves to protect us.
- Yes, people pay more attention and respect us.
- Do you want me to teach you a little ?
- Uh! I will see.
- Ok, as soon as you want, you tell me; OK ?
- OK without fail.

The flight from Sydney to Ayers Rock which is located in one of the 5 states which is Northern Territor, took 3 hours 40 minutes to cover 2837 km. We landed on a ground all red like the clay of the tennis courts at Roland Garros. Visiting Ayers Rock made me very happy; I looked at my iphone for the time, there was a problem: the time kept changing by plus or minus an hour; I did not understand anything.
- Is there a time problem ?
- Is that so ?
- Yes, tell me the exact time.
- You have to change the time: you have to go back 1:30.
- Ah ! Half an hour is the first time I've seen this because usually we only change by hours, not by 30 minutes.
- Hi !

- My iphone does not know the half-hour, damn !
- Why thin ?
- For waking up, so as not to miss the return plane.
- Oh yes it's true ! Well we'll see, okay ?
- OK ! I said.

As we walked around, there were lots of flies, very annoying; I saw a few people who wore a « plague of flies » hat, with threads hanging all around the hat,

Alison explained to me :
- This "bane of flies" hat is to prevent flies from touching faces.
- Ah, good idea !

Here we are near Ayers Rock everything was red, it was amazing! I was thirsty to learn more about the life of the Aborigines.
- Wow, it's high !
- Yes, its height is 348 meters and its altitude above sea level is 863 meters.
- We can go upstairs ?
- I do not recommend it because it is a sacred place for the aboriginal peoples.
- Oh ok ! Where are the aborigines ?
- I've never met one !
- Never ? But the aborigines still live in the middle of nature ?
- Yes and also in the city but they prefer in the middle of nature !
- How do they live? I don't see any houses.

- They live under Ayers Rock, in caves.
- They sleep without a mattress ?
- Unfortunately yes ; many have become deaf.
- What! What do you mean ?
- During the night, they sleep, white grubs enter the ears which pierce the eardrum.
- Ouch! Is it sad and they are receiving care? Doctors or dentist etc ... ?
- There is a volunteer dentist, but who rarely comes; the aborigines take care of themselves but their lives are short, around 52 years.
- Poor people !
- The Aborigines are good at the weather.
- What do you mean ? Tell me more please! I said.
- Up there, an aboriginal scans the weather, he knows if it's going to rain soon or if a cyclone is coming, then he informs the aboriginal people with smoke signals, so that they protect themselves, and we, the whites, we does not know anything. There are therefore more deaths due to natural disasters among whites than among aborigines.
- Wow! The Aborigines are smarter anyway.
- Yes, very fair.
- Why do they prefer to live in the middle of nature ?
- Because the aborigines are not happy in the city, they cannot find work because of a certain

racism if you will; so they drink at the bar and then break everything.
- How do you know that the aborigines break, the whites too !
- I saw it on the television news.
- Pff! Journalists are blah blah; but the problem is that the English killed aborigines and forced them to live like them; this is not possible and we must respect their culture, pff! I rebelled.
- Yes, it's true.
- So can we go around Ayers Rock ?
- Yes it's possible !
- How many km ?
- About 11 km.
- I'm up for it, and you ?
- Me too, we stay together.
- Of course, no worries, and there are kangaroos or spiders or snakes ?
- It's possible, that's why we have to stay close.
- Be careful, you know that I'm not Tarzan hee hee !
- Hi !

At one point, after 6 km, I saw two different courses.
- Which one do we take? I said.
- I follow you !
- Which one have you done ?
- The left one.
- So we take the one on the right, okay ?

- OK no problem.

The path was harder than before, I thought we couldn't get lost or miss the bus, we took a bit of a risk. Suddenly I saw two very cute little aborigines, one of them spoke to me without my understanding.
- Please leave them, we're running away! said Alison, who was afraid.
- Please, stay zen and control yourself, I'm here! I reassured her.
- Ok, I'm trying.
- Wow! They are cute, finally we can see real aborigines.
- Yes wow! said Alison still a little worried.

I said to myself in my thoughts: I understand it because on TV we criticize the aborigines as in the USA we criticize the blacks and, in France, the Arabs; I am not racist.

One of the two spoke to me again, so I answered him in English by mimicking :
- We are deaf and I am French.
- Deaf.
- Yes.
- Plane.
- Yes.

He smiled at me, oh! He was cute, he followed us as if to protect us, we continued on the path, Alison held my elbow, still scared, we crossed the small bridge and there the aborigines stopped their way; I guessed that this place was for the Aborigines only. Alison was relieved and let go of me, but she was too happy to have finally seen Aborigines for the first time in her life, and me too, that was too great.

On the way back to Melbourne by plane via Sydney, I gave a talk on the topic of Uster syndrome in the association "Able Australia" in front of Ushers and deafblind people with Australian sign language interpreters. I first met the manager who was worried about the translations given that I am French and I communicate in French Sign Language (LSF); in fact I can also communicate in Australian sign language (AUSLAN), so we exchanged in AUSLAN, the manager was surprised and reassured; it was thanks to Alison who had taught me this language and of course I had taught her LSF; we communicated in both languages without a problem.

The intervention went well, the Ushers and the deafblind people were happy and they chatted with me with the help of the very happy Alison. A deafblind person offered to visit her equipment showroom, I immediately accepted with pleasure:

in a room, there were technical aids: for example a PC computer connected to a touch screen and a keyboard braille.
- What about the electronic magnifier ?
- I do not know ! I only have simple magnifiers.
- I have the impression that the development of technical aids is lagging behind in France.
- Yes, it's true ! You showed me this device, I have never seen or found it here.
- Ah darn !
- It's the same we can't find an iphone here, it hasn't arrived yet.
- Is that so ! It's weird, yet Australia is not far from the United States.
- Exact !
- It's madness so you have to order abroad through a website to obtain technical aids.
- Yes it's right ! It is not practical ! Alison said.

    The Australian Open had started a few days ago, so Alison and I happily went to watch some second round matches in 38 degree heat in the shade; we saw Monfils, Gasquet, Del Petro, Fish etc, it was a beautiful day and beautiful matches on the fast surface blue pitches, I filmed and photographed, beautiful memories.

    On the way to the southwest of Geelong to go to the seaside at 243 kilometers, Eddy's family, Alison, Ross and I discovered the 12 Apostles, amazing limestone towers that rise to more than 45 meters in the sky. above sea level.

« There were actually 12 apostles, but only 9 there are still standing because of the erosion, »"Alison explains to me.
- That's wonderful ! It looks like Normandy in France! I said.
- I love this place !
- Me too, is there a staircase to go down ?
- Yes over there! Let's go ?
- Yes with pleasure.

Down the cliffs, wow! It was impressive, we strolled by the sea.
The direction of France is located there in the West.

I looked in this direction thinking that I missed France but luckily I had stayed in touch with Stéphanie and with my mother by email, skype and whatsapps, thank you WIFI !! In the rest of the visit, Alison showed me a rock and told me:
- You see this rock, it's an old bridge, the "London Bridge". The arch closest to the edge collapsed on January 15, 1990, trapping two tourists on the forward part. They were rescued by a helicopter, no one was injured during this event.
- Oh damn ! Still, it's scary !
After seeing the apostles on foot, we got back in the car; after a few miles I wanted to check if my photos were good, I yelled and asked Alison:
- Where's my camera ?

- Not seen.

We searched everywhere without success, Alison asked Ross :
- U-turn.
- Why ?
- Sandrine lost her camera.
- Ah darn ! OK.

We turned around, I had the balls because I had taken 1500 photos on my SD card and I prayed that it was found and that no one stole it because there were a few tourists. When they got there, Ross, Eddy and his daughter ran and searched; finally Eddy's daughter found him, nothing was broken phew! I thanked them very much, I was relieved but I did not understand how he had fallen.
- Where did you find it ?
- Near the path over there! said Eddy's daughter.
- Phew! No one had seen or taken it! Alison said.

- Yes that's right and besides it was not easy to spot because it's black in the grass.
- Unbelievable, it did not break in its fall! Alison said.
- Yes it's true, phew and thank you again to you! I tell them.

We continued the tour to Great Ocean Road, and Alison told me the story of the creation of the road :
- In 1919, after the First World War, ex-soldiers returned home and were depressed; the government therefore offered them to build a new road by the sea, they dug the rocks and then created a long road until 1932.
- Wow! It was very hard work since they had no machines.
- What does this place remind you of?
- Uh! It tells me something, I saw it on TV.
- Yes the movie "Mad Max" takes place at this location.
- Wow Super ! That's nice to look at.

   Eddy and I had a swim, the water was fine, it was 35 degrees outside. I said to Alison, in sign language as usual :
- It's still dangerous to swim, you have to be a good swimmer, the sand level is not flat: when you put your feet in the water, the sand sinks, and after two to three no, it goes down suddenly and the waves gain power; there we can drown but further it goes! And to come out, you have to have a good technique following the waves.
- Yes it's right !
- Is it the same everywhere?
- Yes and no, there are a few flat beaches, not many.

- I see it's ideal for surfers.
- Yes, very fair and there was not far from the world championship of surfing.

We flew from Melbourne to Perth in Western Australia, one of 6 states, which is called Western Australia, 3400 kilometers away. We set our watches back two hours. We had completely changed the climate, it was very hot, 42 degrees, and very humid; during the day the temperature can rise to 47 degrees and 27 degrees at night; we sweated a lot, the shoes could have melted, however, the winter is very pleasant, it is not cold. At night, when it's 27 degrees, we sleep with the fan.

We took the road south from Perth, towards Bunbury, a town in the South West, at the corner of Australia, the beach was beautiful, we had a swim, the water was nice, however with the risk of being present sharks; and the prettiest was the sunset. Then to Busselton Jetty the southernmost of Bunbury, we crossed two kilometers on the sea by small train by the longest bridge in Australia, then we went down further on foot to be able to admire the fish and the seaweed under the sea. 'water.

At Perth Harbor, Alison and I took a boat trip to "Rottnest" Island to admire the white sand beach

and also cool off in the appalling heat, 44 degrees; on the island, we booked the bus to go to the most beautiful beach, paying attention to the times, we bathed with caution because of the sharks and we had a picnic; it was a nice cool day, and Alison and I traded :
- From 1838 to 1931 this island was a prison for aborigines, aged 8 to 70 years; this prison contains 3,670 places.
- Oh fuck !! 8 years old is too young, pff! And why only aborigines?
- The English wanted to drive the aborigines to the island.
- It's disgusting and very racist, pff !
- One animal, "the quokka", half rat, half kangaroo, is the only one to live on this island.

It was time to return to the port, unfortunately the buses were disorganized, so we ended up on foot at full speed; we passed two tourists who were cycling, unfortunately one of the two bikes was punctured due to the heat, the tire had melted. Phew, we did not take the wrong path, and arrived safely at the port and then in Perth.

For my last day, it was still very hot, 44 degrees, suddenly the weather changed and became completely black, it announced a very violent thunderstorm, I was worried because soon I was taking the plane to France. Alison whispered to me :

- Please teach me !
- What ?
- Uh! The white cane.
- Ah okay no problem ! Come.
- Great ! she smiles.

In half an hour of class, Alison learned and understood the technique, well done to her !

At Perth Airport, Alison asked for help for me; as I had booked and registered everything, my backpack left. I wanted to recover my passport and my plane tickets, unfortunately the hostess had taken them while saying that the meeting was here in an hour; I was worried about my passport, I checked myself, an hour passed, the hostess returned my passport and my plane tickets; phew! With Alison and then Eddy we hugged each other hard to say goodbye, not a goodbye anyway, hi! Then an escort took me to customs; I got into the plane, as always by the window, but it was dark, pff! I slept soundly between Perth and Dubai because of the heat: for a week it had been over 42 degrees during the day and 27 degrees at night, it had exhausted me.

In Dubai, I waited for a chaperone as usual, there was one who arrived welcoming me to Dubai and then he offered to sit in a wheelchair and my answer was obviously no; he walked me to the waiting room. I spotted an argument between a veiled woman with one leg missing in a wheelchair and 2 customs officers showing her her wooden leg; I guessed that the customs officers refused this wooden leg on the plane because of the screws inside, the woman was panicking because she needed her wooden leg, the discussion lasted a long time, it was not easy.

It was time to get back on the plane, this time for Paris, I sat down again near the window, cool! And I looked at French time, I slept a little longer to catch up with French time straight away. For a while I wanted to go to the bathroom, unfortunately my neighbor was sleeping with a helmet on his ears; I didn't dare wake him up and the second neighbor was awake, so I mimed him to release his seat so that I could step out over the third seat without waking my neighbor. The second neighbor was ok and laughed; given my flexibility, I succeeded without any problem; I stood in line, finally it was my turn; ouch I couldn't open the door, that got on my nerves because in all airplanes the toilet doors are all different pff! So I asked a lady mimicking how do you open? The lady opened the door for me, I thanked her, emptied my bladder and returned to my seat. My neighbor was still sleeping, I was facing the window that dazzled me, I stepped over the first seat and then jumped to my seat, bang! I hadn't seen the headphone wire, so my foot tore it off; my neighbor jumped up and looked at me, me up and standing, and he sitting; I said to myself "shit", I apologized, that I had not done it on purpose and phew! My neighbor smiled at me and the second neighbor was laughing out loud; what a shame !!

Finally the plane landed on French soil after 10:30 p.m. of flight, I turned on my iphone, sent an SMS to Stéphanie to tell her that I had just arrived because she was coming to pick me up at the exit then an SMS to my mother to tell him that I was well in France and alive.

When I left the airport, I finally found Stéphanie after 5 weeks where we had not seen each other, we took pictures of each other with my iPhone. Ah! We saw a lot of difference in skin colors, she white chocolate and me dark chocolate, hey!

While waiting for our TGV, Stéphanie and I chatted a lot, I missed the French signs, we were so happy.

Here I am at home; Stéphanie's husband, Jérôme, had come to pick us up at the station, we ate a French pizza, I told them about my stay until 10:30 p.m., I finally plunged into my real comfortable bed with closed fists.

In the morning, hello laundry, tidying up, and I had to get ready to go to work the next day. Wow! In 5 weeks, I had traveled a total of 46,000 kilometers and taken 2,000 photos, this trip was unforgettable and a good memory. You know that the area of Australia is equivalent to that of Europe and 14 times that of France.

Chapter 11

Spain - August 2012

We had rented an apartment with a pool. I was with nine friends; during the visit, to go to the swimming pool, you had to go down without a ramp; ouch! It was not easy for me, especially the descent, because I could not see the steps of different shapes and also because I did not have a balance. My friend Jérôme accompanied me, informing me as I went along :
- Steps.
- A step.
- Steps...

I was already out of breath because the descent had required a lot of concentration. Jérôme saw that it was not going too well.

A few minutes later, Jérôme called me and showed me :
- I put big stones next to each first step and also at the last steps; can that help you ?
- Ah! It's a very good idea ! Well done and thank you, I'll try it on my own but stay behind me please !
- OK no problem.

I have successfully moved on my own, but still with balance issues. Jérôme's wife, Stéphanie, warned me :
- Walk slowly and take your time ok !
- OK !

It worked, I moved slowly with success; thanks to Jerome's big stones, I felt free; I thanked them.

One afternoon, Jérôme suggested that we go to a nightclub in the evening and I replied :
- You're kidding ?
- No, I'm serious !
- But I can't see anything at night.
- I know, but we'll be there to guide you.
- Uh! OK ! I replied.

Deep inside me it scared me because I hate the dark; but you have to try once to see how it goes and also you have to trust Jérôme as well as Stéphanie.

In the evening, when it was time to go to the nightclub, Jérôme accompanied me, informed me of the obstacles; it was as if I saw like the others thanks to his detailed information; that reassured me. In the nightclub, I saw almost nothing at all, only little flashing lights; suddenly someone came up to me to chat, I wondered who it was. I was stuck, so I told her I was deaf and then visually impaired; and suddenly she's gone.

I was surprised a woman was interested in me, but she fled when she found out that I was deaf and visually impaired. Oh ! She judged too quickly and did not try. Still, it's like racism; pff! I was really disappointed....

It went well although it was a bit long for me due to the fatigue. But it was a good memory!
At the Dali museum, during the visit, Stéphanie asked me :
- Look at this table and take your time!
- OK ! I see pebbles of different sizes, nothing more.
- OK ! I'll give you a hint; OK ?
- OK !
- There it looks like a mouth; so focus on finding out the rest!
- OK .... Ah! The mouth, there the eyes, there the nose....
- That's right.
- Yeh! Thanks for your help.
- And there what do you see ?
- I see a sofa.
- Then ?
- Uh nothing more !
- Ok, there you see a sofa, on the right you look slowly upwards and a little to the right !
- Ah! A painting.
- Yes perfect and it's the same on the left side up.

- Ok... Ah! Another painting like the one on the right.
- Very just ! Then higher !
- Uh... Ah! Curtains.
- Yes exactly !
- So a sofa, two badly placed paintings etc..., what does that mean? I didn't understand why this ?
- Ok I'll give you some clues then you imagine. OK ?
  - OK !
  - Sofa in place of red lips, two frames in place of eyes ...
  - Oh ok !
I re-visualized and at the same time I imagined.
- Ah yes ! Her hair is curtains, her nose is a table, her eyes are two paintings, and her mouth is the sofa.
- Yes exactly !
- Wow! It is well done ! It's impressive !

Deep down I was glad I got to see what it was! It is important that a guide explains well by giving specific additional information or clues etc ... so that I see, imagine or guess like everyone else. I felt that an obstacle had been removed from me; I felt good and above all it made me thirsty to discover lots of things.

Jérôme is a fan of Dali, he gave me a summary about Dali :

- Dali was born in 1904 in Figueras not far from here; he was very talented in art, but the problem was that academics did not accept him because he did not follow the classical methods of art; he invented the paranoid-critical method, he continued to work until his first successes and then became very famous like the great painters.
- It looks like Picasso but the ideas are different, Picasso has his « drawer » styles and Dali has his « reflex » styles.
- Almost yes and you will read on the internet.
  At one point, Jérôme asked me:
- What do you see ?
- Uh! Wait, I concentrate. OK.
  A minute later, I slapped him on the arm because he had played a prank on me; he loves to play pranks, like me !
- It's a red hose reel with a fire hose for museum security.
- Well done !
  I had a good laugh, I always loved his pranks and it made me feel good because before, I had concentrated a lot, it tired me and, there, it was like a break. I felt relaxed to regain energy and strength, the visit continued and went well.
  We rode the catamaran all day in the sun, it was very nice. At the break we had a swim, I swam to a rock; Jérôme helped me to climb almost to the top at five meters; I wanted to dive, it

was my passion before, but now I felt stuck because I couldn't see the depths well; luckily Jérôme was there very close to me, he guided me :
- You're diving there !
- Please explain to me what's around !
- To the right there are low rocks, and to the left there is not enough depth.
- Oh ok ! Please place my shoulders to indicate the precise place to dive.
- OK ! Take your time and wait until you are ready.
- OK !

Jérôme has placed my shoulders well; and it was time to dive, I launched into the dive, my challenge had been met.

I was like: if Jerome hadn't been there, I don't know if I would have? If I had, I might injure myself; but I did not want to take risks. It's wiser and I have to take responsibility for being deprived of things based on my visual problems. In fact, the guide is essential for me to protect myself and also to meet my challenges thanks to complete information and very precise details.

One evening, at the table outside, I had brought a projector that Jérôme installed behind me so that I could help myself at mealtime and also communicate in French Sign Language. At one point Jerome spoke to me a little out of the light, and I often answered off topic; I thought I understood, and not at all, but I didn't understand why. Stéphanie asked Jérôme to stand in the place where the light was strong, he repeated to me what he had said and I answered correctly because, Jerome's skin being well tanned, he had to is placed in a very bright place.

The color of the skin plays for the contrast, and that is very important.

Chapter 12

India - October 2012

I'm not telling you the whole trip. I flew to Asia with my friend Stéphanie who guided me in the middle of a group of hearing people. My eyesight has declined a lot and also my visual field has narrowed further, so I made the decision not to travel on my own; so I preferred to have an experienced guide to be able to continue traveling, my passion.

During the transfer to London airport, to customs, before passing the controller, the latter stopped me by miming with his finger :
- Wait please ! Take off your shoe !
- Sorry ! Should I take my shoes off? Oh there ! It stinks !

The controller was restraining himself not to laugh, he smiled and repeated, mimicking :
- Come on! Take off your shoes and put them on the treadmill.
- OK !
I took off my shoes and then put them on the treadmill, mimicking :

- Oh dear, it stinks !!

The controller wanted to laugh but he smiled, nodding his head; so I went to the control gantry but the controller stopped me again by miming:
- Take that off! By indicating the middle of my body with his finger .
- Sorry ! Do you mean my belt ?
- Yes, put her on the treadmill !
- Oh no ! My pants will fall off, it's not possible.

The controller wanted to laugh too much but he controlled himself well, that was his job; so I took off my belt, while holding the top of my pants, and put it on the treadmill, and I went to the porch; finally I had managed to get through by holding my jeans up; my friend laughed and of course a few people did too. The controller mimed me:
- You can put your shoes and belt back on.
- Phew! Thank you !!

First I put my belt back on, mimicking my jeans like a clown, then my shoes and wanted to grab my little backpack; alas! The controller ordered me :
- I have to empty your bag, please !
- Oh that's not true ! Why me ? I exclaimed in thought.

Ah! Stephanie's bag must also be emptied; phew! I am not the only one.

The controller emptied my bag then returned to another room to check my bag with a more po-

werful scanner and after a few minutes came back and returned my bag to me; I answered him by mimicking :
- No, you have to put things back in place because I am visually impaired.

The controller shut up and put everything back in place; finally everything was settled.

I told myself that customs were very strict, that it was quite normal because of the terrorists. But why me ? Did I look like a terrorist or a thug because of my dark skin or my white cane? I was asking myself these questions. It was okay, the main thing was that everything was going well; but still, it annoyed me. Fortunately, Stéphanie was there to help me ...

One evening, at the restaurant, I sat down at a rectangular table; it was a self-service, there were too many people in line; Stéphanie and I discussed to find a solution :
- It is better that you stay at the table because I cannot at the same time guide you and carry two trays.
- Can I carry a tray ?
- Sorry, it's not easy with so many people: you might run into someone or knock over your board etc.
- Oh yes, it's true, I have no choice, ok !!

Stéphanie went to see the dishes at the self-service, she came back to tell me about the different menus and then I made my choice, she left to have the meal for me, then she returned to help herself to a dish.

While waiting for my meal, I saw that the people were very agitated.

It's still embarrassing for me, it looks like I'm lazy or queen hee !! NO this is a very good solution and there is no choice, otherwise it is a mess and also it is dangerous. I fully assume this situation without feeling embarrassed ...

One day, at the table, everyone was eating and suddenly the lights went out; ah! We were completely in the dark, I continued to eat without any problem because I didn't want my meal to cool down and also because it might be a bit long before having light again. Ah! there, the lights were back on, and I had already finished eating; I looked around the table, I noticed that Stephanie had also emptied her plate like me; it didn't bother us to eat in the dark; people looked at us from top to bottom and were surprised that our clothes were always clean because in the dark they had heard that we continued to eat with the sound of forks and knives wondering how we had eaten in the dark.

On the bus, the guide gave Stéphanie information that she translated into French Tactile Sign Language (in the hand) :
- We are going to visit a temple with a thousand steps, the guide advises you not to go up.
- What! Oh no ! I go like everyone else and why do I not recommend going ?
- He told me that the thousand steps are different from each other and dangerous in the light rain.
- But you are there to guide me; Is it a problem for you ?
- Not at all.
- So here we go and, if I don't feel comfortable, I'll stop and wait until you finish the visit to the top; we will work it out but I want to go all the way.
- OK no problem ! It's perfect.
- Thank you.

To go up, the steps did not pose a problem for me because I could see them well while always looking down to locate the unstable steps; I often needed to take breaks because I was out of breath, or to stretch my thighs and catch my breath because it required a lot of physical work and balance and especially a lot of concentration to avoid falling or falling. hurt myself. While walking, Stephanie informed me if there was a ramp, steps, or not; It really helped me save time or else I wouldn't have made it, I wouldn't have had time.

Here I am at the top, I had succeeded in my challenge, I was so happy but very exhausted. The descent was different, less breathless but very risky because I could not see the steps anymore for lack of contrasts and also because they were slippery; I therefore had to go there very carefully; Stéphanie told me each time the unstable or stable steps and the ramp etc ...
Yeh! I had completed my challenge without falling or hurting myself thanks to Stéphanie; his information had been very important and precious, it had replaced my eyes and I had been able to live like everyone else; and the guide congratulated us.

During the visits to temples, even if they were rather very dark, I was able to admire them thanks to Stéphanie because she informed me in French Tactile Sign Language, with very precise details, on everything she saw, which then transformed into an image in my brain; it's as if I saw like everyone else.
On my return to France, during the transfer to London, Stéphanie told me in LSF Tactile :
- The time is not showing for Paris.
- Is that so ! This is weird !
- Yes we are still waiting a bit.

- Okay !

A few minutes later, it still wasn't posted, it worried us and I said to Stéphanie:
- It is better to ask someone in our group to find out more.
- OK !   I'm looking for someone ... Ah there, come on !

I was still holding her elbow, Stéphanie chatted with a lady and then announced :
- Ah!   There are strikes in Paris, so we don't know what time the plane leaves.
- Oh ! It's not true pff !
- Yeah !
- I hope we don't miss our TGV.
- Oh yes it's true and at what time does our TGV leave ?
- Around 6 p.m.
- Please, precisely ?
- Wait, I'm looking for our tickets, there you are, at 6:14 pm, it's the last TGV; if we miss it, we must leave the next day.
- Ouch !
- My fingers crossed that the theft will be announced soon.

The wait was painful as we still did not know the departure time. Two hours later, finally our flights were announced, phew! But for the TGV?

During the flight, Stephanie and I calculated with the schedule change; ouch! We had very little time left to take our TGV, about ten minutes;

and, going through customs, picking up our suitcases could be long, plus the trip to the wagon; we thought we would do our best to catch our TGV.

On arrival at the airport in Paris, we rushed out of the plane, we walked at full speed to customs; luckily the customs were empty of people; we rushed to collect our suitcases; luckily my suitcase was out first, then Stéphanie's was the fifth.

We were saved; I was holding Stephanie's elbow with one hand and my suitcase in the other; we walked very quickly, zigzagging between people; we were running like crazy but without bumping into each other, not like rugby anyway !

When we arrived at the platform, luckily the controller was there to show us our car, just in front of us; we had been lucky and above all we had managed to catch our TGV; two minutes later the TGV left. Phew !!!

What an adventure !!

Chapter 13

Belgium - 2014

I left very early, first in Rennes to see my friend Anne, then in Belgium with my friend Usher Albert Snaek; my friend Stéphanie accompanied me to Poitiers train station as far as the reception of the disabled. For the first time, an SNCF attendant was going to guide me from the reception to the wagon; at the reception desk for the disabled, the controller asked me, and Stéphanie translated me into French Tactile Sign Language :
- Have you booked Access Plus ?
- Yes.
- Your tickets please !
- Here are my tickets.
- Thank you and wait a bit, let me check and then confirm.
- OK !
- Everything is recorded, someone will come and pick you up to accompany you to your seat.
- How does it work when changing TGV in Paris ?

- In Paris You have to stay in your place, someone will come and pick you up and then accompany you to your seat on the other TGV.
- How will I recognize the person accompanying me ?
- Uh! There is "SNCF" on the T-shirt.
- It's not obvious: I don't see it and the easiest way would be to have a garment with a single color for the SNCF, for example a color either blue or dark red that is the symbol of the SNCF.
- That's true and I'll let the manager know.

It was the time of my departure for Rennes, an attendant, rather a controller, given her outfit, arrived; Stéphanie and I hugged each other :
- Have a nice trip to Rennes then to Belgium and say hello from me.
- Ok without fail and we'll text each other without any problem.

The attendant took me to my seat and then I texted Stephanie :
- It went well ; all is well, the TGV is leavin.
- Great ! I am happy and have a good trip, see you later !

In Paris, I followed what I was told at the counter in Poitiers: I waited in my seat, everyone got out of the TGV, everything was empty around me, I began to wonder where was the guide? A few

minutes passed, it was not possible! Finally I got ready to get off the TGV with my backpack and my white cane to reach the platform; I saw that the platform was almost empty, except for two men, I asked them :
- Where is the guide ?
- I do not know ! Ah, there he is !
- Ah ! Thank you.

The two men, unhappy, discussed with the guide, he apologized and then accompanied me to the other TGV for Rennes, to my seat.

I thought: oh there there! I was afraid of missing my TGV because of the attendant's delay. So, in Rennes, when the TGV stops for five minutes, I won't wait in my seat, I prefer to get off on my own to avoid problems or leave for Brest; no thanks ! Then on the platform, normally my friend Anne should be waiting for me in front of the car because I gave her the numbers; Well ! I'll see and stay ZEN !

In view of the time, I would soon be arriving in Rennes; I got up to grab my backpack, grabbed my white cane, and walked down the hall; it was not easy because the TGV was still moving, it was moving, so I was losing my balance, I was very careful to avoid hitting people seated; phew !

Here I am at the exit door, just as the TGV was stopping; I immediately saw my friend Anne right in front of me, I was relieved, we kissed and then I looked right, left, and I said to Anne :
- Pff ! Where is the guide ?
- Not here, have you booked Access Plus ?
- Yes, in Paris there was a problem, the guide arrived late and I can't see him here, oh !
- Ah darn ! Ah there it is !

I saw a controller running; she found me thanks to my white cane and she said to me then Anne translated me into Tactile (in the hands) :
- Excuse me ! I got the wrong car number, I was at number 5 but no it was number 15.
- Even so, this TGV only stops for five minutes !!
- Yes I know.
- Imagine that I remained in my seat, the TGV would have already left for Brest, I would have died of anguish; it is not possible, I am deaf and very visually impaired, it is not obvious.
- Yes I know, excuse me !
- Next time, pay more attention to deafblind people !
- Yes !
- And there is also a communication problem: you don't know sign language, that's a shame, it's important to reassure people who are deaf and visually impaired; it's not easy for them

and even for me, and besides, I don't know who is accompanying ?
- Ah yes ! It's true, I hadn't thought of that and what should be done ?
- The easiest way would be to wear unique blue or dark red outfits specific to the SNCF, the same for the whole of France so that you can easily find your way around.
- I take note and I will inform my manager.
- OK, thanks.
- Again, my apologies; thank you, see you soon and goodbye.
- Goodbye.
- Anne congratulated me and I thanked her for translating.

Oh ! It's incredible, I don't understand because SNCF has created Access Plus for disabled people, I can't find much suitable. Pff! France is always late! I hope SNCF will do better and better, but that would surprise me; it's still just blah, pff !

A few days later, I had to take the TGV to Belgium but only to Lille Europe, after my brother-in-law Olaf had to pick me up to go by car to Tournai, in Belgium, then my deaf Belgian friend Usher Albert me. would accompany to Liège by train. Anne had to accompany me to my seat because the handicap counter only opens at 7:30 am, but my TGV left at 6:00 am; it was still dark.

When I arrived in Lille Europe, I got off the TGV, I still couldn't see a guide.
Oh that's not possible! pff! Fortunately, I know Lille station well, since I lived 29 years in the North; Well ! I managed with my white cane to go to the Information Point where my brother-in-law Olaf and I had arranged to meet.

First I texted Olaf to let him know that I had arrived at the station and that I will meet him at the Information Point. My iPhone vibrated, I was able to view the text using the built-in magnifying glass; it was a text message from Olaf :
- Sorry, I'm late, I'm still on the road because of traffic jams.
- Ah! Okay, I'll wait for you at the Information Point. Ok, see you later.

I found the Information Point, waited a few minutes, my iPhone vibrated and I read Olaf's text message :
- Where are you ? I am at the Information Point.
- Ah! Me too but I don't see you and you see me ?
- No, I don't see you; wait, I'm looking for you; OK ?

I thought to myself: this is weird; then there are two Information Points? I saw Olaf, I waved at him, not like crazy though ! Phew! He had seen me. Well yes, there were indeed two Information Points at Lille Europe station; luckily we were able to communicate by SMS. Phew! And now on the way to Tournai station in Belgium to join my Belgian friend Albert Snaek. On the road, I texted Stephanie, Albert, Anne and my mother to tell them that everything was fine despite everything.

At Tournai station, I found Albert and we hugged each other with the joy of reuniting.

Another train journey; it was going to last three hours! We were going all the way to Liège and we chatted a lot on the train. It was my first stay at Albert's.

Liège in the rain, it was really like in the North of France.

I took Albert's elbow to guide me, he used his white cane; and here I am at his place, in his apartment, after a long trip and I was exhausted.

The first stay with the Liege lasted four days !

A little story about Liège :

The city of Liège is located 40 kilometers west of Aachen (Aachen) in Germany, 30 kilometers north of Maastricht in Holland and 100 kilometers east of Brussels, the capital.

Liège is a very old city that already existed in Roman times and Liège was for a long time a principality ruled by the prince bishop of Liège, from the Middle Ages to the French revolution.

Liège is also called the city of a hundred spiers because there are many churches, cathedrals and collegiate churches.

We also call Liège, the fiery city, from the name of a novel that tells the story of the city of Liège!

Liège is the friendliest city in Wallonia and the people of Liège are known for partying, drinking Péket, a Belgian alcohol specialty, and eating fries with meatballs in hunter sauce.

Liège is still the birthplace of Georges Simenon, famous author of detective novels! Liège is also a crossroads between Germanic culture and Latin culture.

On the first day, Albert showed me around Liège. We were each walking around with our white canes and it was not right at all because our own white canes kept crossing and blocking us due to our different sweeping rhythms and the lack of synchronization between us. There was only one possible solution: one would use the white cane to provide security and find the way, and he would guide the other holding his elbow. With our technical guide experience and Albert's knowledge of the city of Liège, it worked! Yeh !

Albert told me the story of the cathedral, which can no longer be seen on Place Saint Lambert because it was destroyed during the Liège revolution. But we can still see the old pillars of this disappeared cathedral, surrounded by iron fences to protect them.

Saint Lambert's Square saw the horror with 10 dead, near the court: there is a small elevated esplanade where a killer fired shots at people waiting for the bus. I had seen him on the television news.

Here is a staircase of 374 steps called the mountain of Bueren and with an average slope of almost 28%.

Liège is a very rewarding large city with a historic past and ancient heritage.

On Monday morning, we were walking quietly in the pedestrian district in the center of Liège, Albert was using his white cane, then suddenly an orange construction van came towards us, I pulled Albert's elbow for us move to the side, but Albert refused and we continued straight ahead. I was a little scared, then I wanted to laugh too much because the van had to back up to avoid us. I then pulled Albert's elbow to tell him that was enough; I couldn't help but laugh. Finally we changed direction by going to the side and the van left.

We burst out laughing like crazy in each other's arms and I said :
- But are you crazy and you dare to do that ?
- Well, we're Usher, so priority, like the rhino; free to walk in the pedestrian area !
- Yes but all the same, we can see a little; but it's funny; I didn't think the van would have backed up anyway oh! Hihihi !

Albert doesn't always pay attention! When arriving at the pedestrian crossing to cross the road, Albert looked at the pedestrian lights and I looked at the cars to my left.
Just as the pedestrian light turned green, Albert wanted to cross, I pulled him because a car had burned the red light. We educated each other well to protect each other.

During a break, Albert and I sat outside outside a bar to sample various beers; Albert stopped me from drinking, telling me :
- Be careful there are wasps !
- Or ? I do not see them.
- I'll help you hunt them.
- OK, thanks ; I did not think that in Belgium there were wasps.
- In summer, there are plenty of wasps because of the beer which attracts them.

Deep inside me, oops! And luckily Albert was there or else I would have been stung, so I might be dead; it is not easy !

You know that in Belgium there are over a thousand different beers!
On Sunday, with Albert's parents, we visited the countryside in the Liège region. We first went to visit the Abbey of Val Dieu in the Pays de Herve, well known for its orchards, cheeses, beers, Herve syrup and apple juice.
We had an Abbey beer at 11 am with the cheese.

Then we visited a tower (Belvedere) that looks like a lighthouse and the place is called Les Trois Frontières because the borders of Germany, the Netherlands and Belgium meet there. Albert offered to go upstairs; I'm always up for it because I love to see the sights and the landscapes, I noticed that Albert was worried about me; So I asked him :
- It's okay ?
- Yes, but pay attention to the steps and use your white cane too, please.
- Oh ! I know how to climb the stairs ! Hi !
- It's slippery because it's still raining, and also it's narrow.
- Do not worry. OK !

I climbed without difficulty; Here I am at the top, the view was magnificent despite the rain and a little fog making the view less beautiful; but we had no choice and it was better than nothing. We took pictures, and I was waving: over there it's the Netherlands, over there it's Belgium and over there it's Germany.

You can see the city of Aachen from the top of the tower.

Further on there is a landmark where the three borders meet and you can put one foot in Germany, the other foot in the Netherlands and one hand in Belgium.

Here is also the highest point in the Netherlands; it rises to 300 meters.

Afterwards, we went to the Belgian Ardennes to visit the highest point in Belgium which is 700 meters away and which is located in a natural park called the Hautes Fagnes. The Hautes Fagnes are heathlands, peat bogs and forests.

I had a delicious ham on the bone at the restaurant in Botrange with Albert and his family. Albert was kind to help me carve the ham.

We ended the day at Albert's parents with some delicious pancakes.

On Monday we did the shopping for the return to France the next day. At the supermarket, we went to the liquor department to buy a bottle of Péket because in France we don't find any, so I took advantage of it. But a store clerk pushed Albert, nearly knocking him to the ground, and Albert screamed to tell him that we were there with our white canes. The employee didn't care and ignored us! I had never seen this in my life! We were rushed because the employee wanted to put bottles back on the shelf, he was in a hurry and we weren't moving. Albert would take the bottles of peket one by one and explain to me in tactile sign language the taste of each bottle.

We went to the cash register to pay for the groceries and Albert told me to look under the conveyor belt; I didn't quite understand, so he explained to me :
- To pay for the races in cash, we put the tickets or change in slot machines below the conveyor belt.
- Oh okay, this is the first time I've seen this.
- It is not suitable for visually impaired and blind people.
- Yes, it's true ! Oh that's nonsense! What are you doing then.
- I give the cashier and she has to bend over and bend over to put the money in the machine.
- Oh my, it's not practical.
- What to do ? And we have no choice.
- I don't understand why they're doing this ?
- To prevent the cashier from stealing the money or making mistakes !

- Ah, that's why; but it is not suitable for visually impaired and blind people.
- Here !

It was my last day, we were shopping to buy souvenirs especially Belgian chocolates like the Leonidas brand which I love. Albert explained to me that there are several brands of Belgian chocolates: Léonidas, Galler ...

To return to France, at the Bruxelles-Midi station, we sought assistance to accompany me to the train.

Albert does not know the Bruxelles-Midi station well because it is very big, complicated and he never goes there. He prefers Brussels-Central or Brussels-North, smaller stations.

We have found a special terminal for disabled people; unfortunately, you had to press a button to call and speak into the hygiaphone; but since we are deaf, it was therefore not possible.

We went to the Thalys Information Point, and Albert explained to the employee that I had booked the assistance. The employee asked to come back half an hour before the train left and that she would call for assistance at that time.

We went for a coffee and a sandwich for lunch.

Albert told me to look for the official meeting place with assistance, for himself if he came to France the following year.

We knew we had to go back to the Thalys information office at 11:30 am. When we arrived at the Thalys information office, the office was closed and the employee was missing.

We panicked to another office to check in the luggage, to tell the clerk that we were deaf and that I needed help getting to the train car. The baggage clerk said we had to call the kiosk, but Albert explained that was not possible because we were deaf and visually impaired.

The porter called to inquire and asked us to wait 5 minutes. Then the employee came out of the office, took my bag and guided me; but Albert, who had to follow by himself with his white cane, could not follow the employee who was walking very quickly. Luckily Albert knew the platform number.

Fortunately, before getting into the wagon, I saw "second class", I thought to myself: no, I'm in first class; So I said to Albert:

- No, he got the wrong car, I should be in first class.
- Is that so ! Wait, I'll tell him.

Albert asked the guide :
- Excuse me, check the tickets, she booked first class, not second class !

But Albert couldn't stay on the train and he got out.

Suddenly, the guide left without listening to me; he had gone to look for Albert on the platform to act as an interpreter because he had a communication problem.

Albert translated for me what the attendant asked: he wanted to see the tickets to know what mistake he had made !

Albert quickly got angry, he was anxious and I too was worried because when the TGV changed to Paris, an attendant had to look for me at my seat and since it would not be the right number, it was messing around.

Phew! I moved into first class with relief. Oh there ! Belgian assistance was inadequate and Albert was embarrassed; I reassured him it wasn't his fault.

A year later, I went to join Albert for the second time in August 2015. I was with my sister Frédérique who lives in the North, near the Belgian border. My mother, my sister and I had left the North by car to go to Tournai station where I quickly found Albert and his friend. We hugged and I introduced him to my sister Frederique and my mother. It was time to go, my sister and mom were heading back north and I had spotted my red suitcase, so it was good.

Hop! We were on the train and we were settling down when Albert told me :
- Why three bags ?

- No, two bags! I told him without thinking because of the fatigue.

In the train, we exchanged together in a good atmosphere and with joy. Later I thought about what Albert had told me about the three bags so I rechecked, spotted my red suitcase and my purse and then a third bag that must have belonged to my friend. 'Albert. So it was good mmmhhh! And that was okay, I let it go. We changed stations in Brussels to take the train from Liège and we joined Albert's friend's husband on the platform. We met.

On arrival in Liège, these friends accompanied us to Albert's apartment. I headed to the bedroom to drop off my purse and Albert brought my red suitcase and a bag; I told him :
- This bag is your friend's, not mine.
- Yes, it's your bag, it's your sister who gave it to me.
I was surprised and found it weird.
Albert's friend joined us in the bedroom and I dared to ask her :
- Is that your bag ?
- No, it was your sister who gave it to me.
- Ah darn ! Really it's not mine! I sighed !

Well ! I still opened the bag like a nosy to understand and find out who owned this bag !! I opened it up and saw a pool ball, a large towel and a large bra !! I guessed it was my sister and she was wrong.

Pff ! We had come with his bag for nothing but the problem was I didn't know when I was going to be able to return it to him? Oh fuck! But we burst out laughing. I texted my mom and called my sister by FaceTime to tell her that her pool bag was in Liège! My sister was furious and I repeated to her that she was the one who gave her bag to Albert's friend! So we negotiated to find a solution so that she could go and collect her bag! Finally we made an appointment at the Brussels-Midi station while I will transit to return home.

In the evening, Albert and his friends suggested that I go to the house for the deaf, which only opens Tuesdays from 6 to 11 p.m. and I told them ok despite the fatigue caused by the trip.

The Liège home for the deaf is the oldest home for the deaf in Europe! It is over 100 years old. There is a museum on the history of the deaf upstairs.

On Wednesday Albert offered me a boat trip to admire Liège and also the banks of the river, the Meuse.

The Meuse has its source in France, then crosses Belgium and flows into the sea in Amsterdam.

Of course I was up for it, Albert showed me the different buildings etc ... In the evening, Albert's friends came to dine at the apartment and while Albert was preparing the aperitif his friend asked me to signing :
- What did you visit today?
- Liège by boat, uh! Unfortunately Albert fell into the water! I told him !

His friend jumped worried and went to Albert to ask him how he had managed to fall into the water. I secretly laughed and a few minutes later his friend came back and patted me on the shoulder.
I was laughing to death; I had had it; We laughed.
His friend's wife arrived later and asked me the same question as her husband.
Obviously I answered the same, she jumped up in concern and went to find Albert. A few minutes later, she came back naively and we had a good laugh together again! Poor friends! I loved the Belgians.
On Thursday, we visited Namur which is located on the Meuse, 50 km from Liège. We went there by train. Albert showed me the university where he studied biology as well as his old university room ! It is a charming old town with old alleys and nice shops.
Namur is the capital of Wallonia and there is in Namur the only bilingual French-LSFB (Belgian

French Sign Language) school that Albert showed me.

Albert and I went to visit the citadel which offers a beautiful view of the city of Namur and the valleys of the Meuse and Sambre.

But the stairs are difficult to climb because the citadel dates from the Middle Ages. To go down, we were miraculous because the steps were uneven, high and slippery !

At one point Albert was tactfully explaining something to me on the sidewalk and suddenly a guy rushed past us while we were communicating in LSFB with our four hands !

Without embarrassing myself, I shouted :
- I finally !
- What ?
- You're cutting our conversation!   said Albert speaking !
- Bah! You get in the way by blocking the sidewalk !
- You could warn us and apologize for passing or you could make a detour! said Albert !

This guy left without apologizing, pff!   What rude !!

On Friday we went to Maastricht in the Netherlands; here is a bit of history :

The city of Maastricht is located in the center of the province of Limburg in the Netherlands. As the capital of the province it has 122,000 inhabitants. The Belgian border is to the west of the city, the Meuse is bordered by Lixhe on the left bank and Maastricht on the right bank. Lixhe, one of the oldest towns in the Netherlands, was attached to the city.

Maastricht means "bridge over the Meuse"! It is the oldest bridge in the Netherlands and dates back to Roman times !

We were going on the Vrijthof which is the largest square in the city.

In the square, the Catholic Cathedral is next to the Protestant Church.

It was beautiful to see !

We walked around; there was no car, that was cool.

At noon Albert suggested that I go eat at the Maastricht Mill. It dates from the 13th century and is still in operation. The mill grinds the flour, it is supplied to the bakery which bakes the bread for the restaurant and we really enjoyed ourselves.

Maastricht, you have to pay attention to the tracks reserved for bikes !

We once wanted to cross at a zebra crossing but there were no pedestrian lights and suddenly a cyclist suddenly stopped right in front of us.

We swerved to avoid the accident anyway and then asked ourselves who in Holland had priority between pedestrians and bicycles? Fortunately the white cane had protected us well.

On Saturday a friend of Albert drove us in his car to visit the site of the Battle of Waterloo where Napoleon was beaten! In June 2015, we celebrated 150 years of the Battle of Waterloo! There is a huge hillock that you have to climb to admire the beautiful view as well as the famous Waterloo lion. There is a museum with the reconstruction of the Battle of Waterloo.

At noon, we had lunch at the bottom of the hill.

In the afternoon, we went to visit the Hergé museum where Tintin's collections and comics are exhibited; Albert helped me a lot and translated what I couldn't read; it was wonderful to visit.

On Sunday Albert and I went to Verviers for lunch at noon with Albert's parents.

Albert said to his mother :
- Sandrine likes panties !

Albert's mum didn't understand, but Albert's dad repeated to her :
- Sandrine likes speculoos.

In fact, Albert had badly articulated: to say speculoos he had said panties. They burst out laughing without my understanding; Albert told me all about it, and I laughed myself.

At noon, we had a great meal with mussels and fries made by Albert's father; it was so delicious!

Albert's parents drove us back to Liège; on the way we stopped at Banneaux where the Blessed Virgin appeared! It's like Lourdes, but in Belgium!

Monday, the last day, was rest, we did the shopping for the return trip and walked around Liège again !

We drank Péket at Maison du Péket! In the evening, the friends who had accompanied us from Tournai train station came for supper!

It was my return to France and we were at the Bruxelles-Midi station.

As my sister had got the bag wrong, so I had a date with her! We had arranged to meet at the Info Point, but my mobile phone (SMS, in French) was not working (no network) and we had to wait an hour and a half because my sister was waiting at the other Info Point! We were going to ask to make a general call to find my sister when she saw us after looking everywhere for us.

Phew! I had given him the bag back, I was sure I wasn't leaving with it.

It was still the same problem for the accompaniment, as last year, nothing had changed, and we did like last time.

For support, Albert asked the Thalys Info Point for help, the employee took the information about me and told us that the guide would come at 11.30 am. The attendant never came. We went to the platform because it was in the same place and at the same time as last year.

Pff! The attendant was on the platform and Albert yelled at him for his lack of seriousness.

I settled in well, the TGV left; after a few minutes someone tapped me on the shoulder; automatically I thought it was the conductor, I rummaged to hand him my train tickets. But he was not a controller because I saw his card with the three colors of the French flag; I deduced that he was a policeman; unfortunately I couldn't see anything at all because of the backlighting made by the windows in front of me, but I spotted the policeman's finger raised upwards, I guessed that he wanted me to take out my red suitcase for the search for the fact that a terrorist had wanted to stab travelers in the Thalys three days ago; I had seen the information on the internet. I didn't want to open my suitcase especially to show my dirty panties etc ... So I found a good excuse by telling him that I was deaf by miming my hands over my ears, then I showed him my white cane, to say "blind"; the policeman didn't know what to do anymore, he put his hand on my shoulder to tell me to let go and that it was okay; I sighed and then texted Albert :
- A policeman wanted to search my red suitcase.
- Me too, he wanted to see my little backpack, then he spoke to me, I did not understand a thing.
- I think it was because of the white canes, he thought we were weird; maybe he thought we were false blind because we can see a little; he was suspicious of the terrorists.

- It's possible. Welcome back.
- You too.

    The white cane is not only for the blind, it is also for the visually impaired.

Epilogue

What is USHER syndrome?

It is retinitis pigmentosa associated with deafness.

Retinitis pigmentosa (RP) is a degenerative genetic disease of the retina of the eye that is characterized by progressive and gradual loss of vision, usually progressing to blindness.
On the retina, there are the rods which give night vision and peripheral vision and also black and gray colors, and the cones which allow central vision and also the vision of other colors.

There are three types of Usher syndrome:
Type 1:
- Profound deafness from birth
- Delay in walking, between 16 and 24 months due to balance problems which are gradually compensated for
- Around 7 to 9 years old: Difficulties in night vision
- Around 18 years: progressive reduction of the visual field which continues throughout life

Type 2:
- Moderate to severe deafness at birth
- Difficulties with night vision in early adolescence
- Progressive deterioration of the visual field throughout life

Type 3:
- No deafness at birth. Deafness appears gradually
- First, cone damage (central vision): reduced visual acuity.
- Then attack of the rods: progressive deterioration of the field of vision, difficulties of night vision

Since I was born profoundly deaf, so I have Type 1 Usher syndrome but I don't like to say that, I just prefer to say that I have Usher syndrome.

Currently, my sticks and cones are working less and less because of my age; my visual field has narrowed over time from about 160 degrees to below 5 degrees: unlike you who have 180 degrees, I see as in a rifle barrel (tubular vision) and I give you examples:
- I am completely blind in the evening and at night, and I need a lot of light to see well like everyone else for example, when you use 40 watts, I need more than 180 watts for a room of less than 10 m2.

- I am more and more wrong in the colors and I no longer see the writings in ball-point pen or in wooden pencil; I am therefore obliged to use black markers more than 1 mm thick when making large letters; and I can't read much or more than 15 minutes because it tires me quickly, it hurts my eyes.

- To read mail or magazines at my home, I use a technical aid: a tele-magnifier that allows the letters to be magnified and the colors to be inverted, for example white or yellow writing on a black background, to be less dazzled and make reading more comfortable, but not too long because that tires me quickly anyway.

- For SMS or Private Messages on Facebook etc ..., I use my iPhone or an iPad because, in the parameters, I can adjust the size with a zoom, I can also invert the colors (black screen, white writing) etc... So I can live like you.

- When you are outside in good sunny weather and then come home, your eyesight adapts and you can see normally in less than 30 seconds while for me I need 2 to 3 minutes of adaptation time.

- You can see a photo at a glance, I can't; I see in 15 squares, it means like through a grid of 5 columns and 3 rows for a photo so I have to look at each small square, 15 squares in all, it takes a lot of work to understand what this corresponds to picture ; sometimes I am wrong or have trouble guessing. So, with the help of someone who explains me briefly and shows me where my head is, for example, I can find my way around the photo after several minutes.

- To find an object on the ground, I can't find it quickly like you, I have to lie down on the ground and look patiently, or I use my iPad or my iPhone which help me a lot thanks to the good quality of images; but I don't always find lost items quickly, usually it takes more than half an hour; sometimes it annoys me because of the waste of time and also the patience it takes.

- In a room, I need contrasts to facilitate my movement etc ..., for example a dark sofa that contrasts with a light floor. Also things must be tidy, for example we do not leave the bag lying around anywhere in the hallway, it might drop me or I might crush it....

- In the street, you perceive everything very quickly without problem, me no, I have to watch out for people, bicycles and cars which pass quickly or even slowly; As I move forward I have to spot: the post, the place, the sidewalk, the sign, etc., it's too hard for me, I'll explain why: people move quickly to the right or on the left, I walk slowly, moving my head from right to left to avoid bumping into myself because my visual field is very narrow! It scares me, I don't want to hurt myself or go to the hospital; besides, I can't hear the cars! In fact, I need someone who helps me by accompanying me, it is more reassuring because I have already almost been run over by a car that did not respect the highway code and had burned down the red light and also, another time, by a fire engine or police car with a flashing light, because of my loss of vision and my deafness; and yet I use my white cane! I'm still scared ...

- It's difficult to orient myself with my white cane, I can't hear, I am often clumsy, the posts are not contrasted enough with the ground ... Also I do not see the signs, I am hyperopic and myopic! In addition my visual field is very narrow; if the sun is strong, it dazzles me, or if the weather is gray, if it is dark, I do not see anything, I am afraid of being lost ... So now I have hired a professional to accompany me to go shopping, to go out without shame; so I accept myself and feel safe.

- To be able to go to appointments, for example to the doctor, the dentist ... I use the handibus services to transport disabled people or I take a taxi. I am not ashamed of it, I have no choice and I feel empowered; but it depends where I'm going, sometimes I need more guidance.

- When the postman or the delivery people ring, they want to tell me something, so I immediately take out my iPhone to use the dictation or they show me a piece of paper. I always use my iPhone, I photograph and then I magnify by inverting the colors, if I am not in the sun; That does not bother me; or I'm using Magnifier X30 through my iPhone. If I am in direct sunlight I cannot use my iPhone, it blows my mind too much.

- In a store, when it's written too small, I take a photo on my iPhone, then I can magnify my screen and write white on a black background, which allows me to see better.
- In the shops, the lighting is variable, it is horrible for me because I have difficulty seeing objects, writings; So I have to call a salesperson to help me out but the problem is I can't see who the salesperson is, I'm confusing people and salespeople; and also I can't lip read anymore to understand what people are saying, I can't do it

on my own. I have to call a friend of mine or a professional to accompany me.

- When friends guide me, I walk around with ease, and each time I offer them a gift or a meal or a drink, or I pay for their petrol etc ... it is quite normal to make an exchange of service because they pay petrol, insurance, their vehicles, me nothing, it is necessary to share.

- When I do the housework, at the end I think I have cleaned everything well, unfortunately my family and my friends tell me no; because of my very weak visual field, I cannot see everything 100% well; So I take a household help. And also my friends warn me by telling me that my clothes are full of stains.

- So that I can cook, I have to adapt the kitchen well, for example, install spotlights or LED lighting tiles under the furniture or very clear lights on each place: work board, cooking, dishes ... On the induction hob, I use my iPhone to find the ignition buttons or the timer or the temperature. And by also being careful to have furniture and appliances in contrasting colors, I can cook like you.

Profound deafness is the complete loss of hearing; I therefore do not perceive any sound, I live in silence. I am also losing my balance due to vestibular damage to the inner ear due to Usher syndrome, so I am not walking upright, I am told I am drunk! But no !

Overall, my eyes work 3 times more than yours, it's very hard for me because I get tired quickly now; I need an attendant to make my life easier and also to tire me less.

- To communicate, I practice French Sign Language: LSF is the means of communication for the deaf; but I also have retinitis pigmentosa which causes me to lose another of my 5 senses, vision; So I'm missing 2 of the 5 senses: vision and hearing. I use tactile LSF in the hand, to allow me to understand conversations and also to avoid misunderstandings ...

- In everyday life, it is difficult for me to see the signs, because, if I am too close, I cannot see everything, if I am too far, I cannot see well; so I have to take hands to understand the signs. But with my iPhone or iPad or video magnifier, I can see from a distance what someone is saying to me in Sign Language, because the frame is small, the signs do not go outside the frame; and I can ask the other to come closer or back if I can't see well enough.

- To communicate with people who do not practice LSF, I use dictation via my iPhone; This is very convenient, first I have to explain my deafness and vision problems to them and then I use my iPhone, especially dictation, telling them to speak in front of my iPhone. At first people don't understand what it is for then they see that it helps me understand; and we can converse thanks to dictation; they are reassured, they are less afraid and also it is comfortable.

People with Usher syndrome do not all have the same vision; but, with those who communicate in sign language, it is necessary to put on dark, united outfits, to sign gently at the level of the head, in a restricted space, as in a screen. You need to be well lit and have a dark gray wall behind you.

But nothing prevents me from traveling, I have to look for solutions, for example having experienced guides, although in France there are very few. The problem is also that the law of February 11, 2005 creating the Departmental House for the Handicapped People (MDPH) did not mention anything specific for people with a double sensory handicap suffering from Usher syndrome. So the MDPH automatically gives us the deafness package, as for the deaf. To obtain the blindness package according to the MDPH scales, it takes

1/20 visual acuity after correction; in fact they do not take into account the visual field. This is not fair because in the law to pass the driver's license, you need a visual field greater than 60 degrees in each eye and that, according to the standards of the World Health Organization, when a person has less than 20 degrees of visual field, she is considered blind, like a person who has 1/20 of visual acuity.

But the MDPH does not want to know. In addition, in some departments, the MDPH grants the blindness package to people with Usher syndrome who have less than 20 degrees of visual field, even if they have more than 1/20 of visual acuity.

Summary

Prologue

1 - Greece - 1986
2 - China - 1991
3 - Turkey -1992
4 - South Africa - 1994
5 - South America - 1998
6 - Martinique - 1999
7 - Burundi - 20018
8- Morocco - 2002
9 - Egypt - 2006
10 - Australia in 2011 - 2012
11 - Spain August 2012
12 - India October 2013
13 - Belgium 2014

Epilogue

My thanks to Alison Raison for the corrections on translate, to my family as well as the friends around me for their encouragement!

BOD EDITION November 2020

CPSIA information can be obtained
at www.ICGtesting.com
Printed in the USA
LVHW051127171120
671905LV00005B/81

9 782322 256563